Life on the Rocks

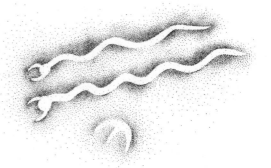

"Star Man" shield bearer. The four-pointed star represents Venus to the Tewa people.

Life on the Rocks

One Woman's Adventures in Petroglyph Preservation

Katherine Wells

University of New Mexico Press | Albuquerque

Library of Congress Cataloging-in-Publication Data

Wells, Katherine.

Life on the rocks : One woman's adventures in
    petroglyph preservation / Katherine Wells.
        p. cm.
    ISBN 978-0-8263-4671-1 (PBK. : ALK. PAPER)
1. Pueblo Indians—Antiquities—Collection and preservation—
    New Mexico—Sandoval County.
2. Petroglyphs—New Mexico—Sandoval County.
3. Picture-writing—New Mexico—Sandoval County.
4. Archaeological surveying—New Mexico—Sandoval County.
5. Vecinos del Rio (N.M.)
6. Sandoval County (N.M.)—Antiquities—Collection and preservation.
I. Title.
    E99.P9W425   2009
    978.9'57—dc22
                            2009003362

The names of some individuals have been changed.

All of the petroglyph drawings in this book were
created by the author.

Book and cover design and type composition by
    Kathleen Sparkes. The text was composed
    using Fontfont Scala OT 10.5/14, 26P.
    Display type is Scala Sans and ITC Officina.

For my son, Tas

Bone, sand, aroma of sorrow
and stillness.
Mother soft sculpture of hills,
sound of the moon's slow rise,
high octaves of light,
impeccable light.

—Katherine Wells

Acknowledgments

Deep gratitude to Jennifer Owings Dewey for constant encouragement and skillful critiques. Without her this book would be in my closet in first-draft form. I thank Diane Carver for early enthusiasm and Jean Gillingwators, Kathryn Wilkens, Lucia Ortiz y Garcia, Angelina Valdéz, Janet MacKenzie, and others for thoughtful readings and suggestions. Some of the people who appear in the book under pseudonyms helped by recalling important details of events I describe. I am grateful to Jane Kramer, whose kind help freed up writing time, my supportive and insightful editor, Lisa Pacheco, and Steven Rudy, my ever-patient computer guru. Without the hard work of many friends, neighbors, and others who care deeply about protecting petroglyphs and community, the story would have ended differently. I thank them heartily.

Author's Note

The term "rock art," used to refer to petroglyphs and pictographs separately or as a combined entity, has long been disliked by many scholars and aficionados as well as Native Americans. Their complaint is that expressions left on rocks by people long ago do not constitute "art" as understood in the modern world. Scholar Joseph Epes Brown tells us that there is "no single term for what we refer to as art" in any Indian language—past or present.

The issue arose at a binational workshop where I was invited to give a presentation in 2007. Called *Set in Stone*, the event focused on petroglyph management in the United States and Mexico and was sponsored by Petroglyph National Monument and the University of New Mexico in Albuquerque. During the sessions several speakers brought up the long contended use of "rock art" as a term. Ed Lee Nate, a member of the Tohono O'odham tribe, made an eloquent appeal for an alternative. He said his people refer to rock art images as "long ago told." The phrase resonates and invokes the living history of rock art. Sadly, it doesn't work well as a noun, but I applaud it as a way to approach the images.

William Breen Murray, former editor of *La Pintura*, a newsletter published by the American Rock Art Research Association, addressed the subject in the December 2005 issue of the publication. He noted that no satisfactory alternate term has arisen in spite of the efforts of many people over the years. Terms such as "rock representations," "rock graphics," and "rock images" have not caught on. "Rock art" persists as the default term.

Scholars and those who care about rock art will continue to wrestle with the problem. In this book I have used the term "rock art" because it is impossible to avoid. If one thinks about the dictionary's first definition of "art" as "skill acquired by experience," then "rock art" does accurately describe the images long ago told.

Katherine Wells

Life on the Rocks

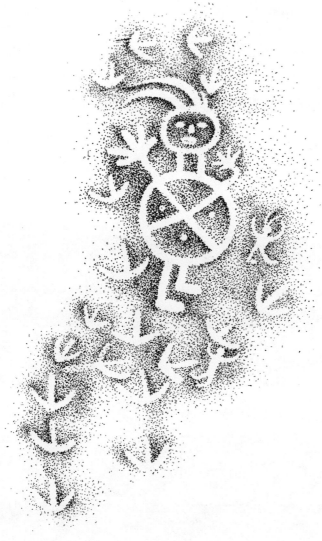

One

The air cooled as we walked past mortared stone walls into the small cliff dwelling eighty feet above the San Juan River in Utah. Welcome relief from the June heat and intense sunlight outside. As our eyes adjusted to the soft interior light, an image of an incised turtle emerged from the smooth coral-colored sandstone of the back wall. I was transfixed by the simple beauty of the glyph. Centuries dissolved. The presence of those who had once lived there was palpable.

Thus began my odyssey into the mysterious realm of rock art. It was the late 1960s when my husband Geza and I and our friends Jean and Joel spotted the cliff dwelling on a rafting trip. We had our own raft and were exploring the San Juan years before commercial rafters began ferrying adventure seekers through the rapids or brightly colored kayaks appeared between the river's canyon walls.

The cliff dwelling appeared not to have been visited since its original inhabitants departed for reasons we will never know. Near the fire pit we found tiny dried corncobs and bits of woven fiber we guessed were from ancient sandals. A few potsherds lay scattered about. Jean had an eight-by-ten-inch spiral notebook in her pack. We borrowed bits of charcoal from the fire pit and made simple rubbings of the turtle image the way we had rubbed a pencil across pennies under a sheet of paper from our Big Chief tablets as school kids. The charcoal obscured the paper's blue lines.

Back home we framed the images and soon began scouring the vast deserts of Southern California for more petroglyphs, armed with materials to make more rubbings. In those days, when few people were aware of petroglyphs, such activity was acceptable. Now those who care about these irreplaceable images on stone make only photographs or sketches. Oils from too many fingers or foreign substances will, over time, damage these gifts from the past and destroy the possibility of someday dating the glyphs.

My fascination with rock art is part of the same impulse that seized Geza and me in the early 1960s when we were first married. On a trip to Arizona we fell in love with Native American basketry and began to collect baskets like people possessed. The wider world of art had not yet "discovered" the Indians, ancient or contemporary, as producers of "high art." Thus we were able to amass a handsome, small collection for a modest amount of money.

The desire to possess fine baskets was like an addiction. I thought about it for hours every day; I planned trips to look for baskets, scanned the Los Angeles Times for ads, and tried to locate more sources to investigate. Geza and I drove all over the West in search of new treasures, spending every long weekend and much of our vacation time on our quest. I still lament not buying some beautiful baskets we passed up because we felt they were too expensive. The beauty and uniformity of stitches in coiled basketry, the obvious care and skill with which they were made, the way they felt in my hands, the sweet aroma of dried willow, reeds, and roots from which they were made, and my imaginings about the women who wove the baskets made them precious.

Back then a good quality early-twentieth-century basket could be had for as little as fifty dollars. Being recently graduated from college with sizeable debts limited our disposable income. In those days fifty dollars was real money compared to today. But Geza and I bought baskets rather than furniture or a house or a fancy car. After a year or two we had forty or fifty fine baskets from the Pomo, Pima, Apache, and other southwest and western tribes, but nary a chair or other piece of furniture. We made do with well-worn pieces provided by our landlady.

Years later I discovered another reason I was attracted to baskets and other Native American art. In the 1990s, long after I became afflicted with petroglyph fever, I learned from an elderly aunt that my paternal great-grandmother was a Cree Indian. Kaziah Jane Brown. Neither my father, grandfather, nor anyone else in the family had ever spoken about her. Before

Katherine Wells

my generation, Indian ancestry, like homosexuality, was kept securely locked in the closet. The news resonated within me like something long lost that I had finally found. I wondered what part of Kaziah Jane had survived within me. Was she the source of my high cheekbones, the reason I'm driven in directions no one else in the family understands?

Elements of my upbringing add another layer to the mystery of my compulsion. The harsh fundamentalist Christian persuasion of some of my mother's family terrified me when I was a small child. One aunt, whom I dearly loved and who was an important part of my life in other ways, implied in her later years that she felt like a failure because she had not "saved my soul." My five-year-old soul froze from her preacher haranguing that I was a born sinner condemned to hellfire. Consequently, I came to adulthood with little in the way of spiritual moorings. For a while I tried being a Presbyterian, but the faith didn't stick. The nature-based spiritual aspects and aesthetics of tribal art and life spoke to me in a way nothing else had.

Many years passed before I became conscious of why rock art appealed so much to me. Most rock art was created as a spiritual activity in relation to its locale in the natural world. A young person on a vision quest might carve a handprint to mark the place he received a spirit helper or a shaman might create a glyph as part of a ceremony to bring rain. My perception of petroglyphs derives from a visceral rather than an intellectual level.

And I am not alone. By now I have met many people I refer to as "rock art junkies." They will drive to the ends of the earth, endure deeply rutted or muddy roads, suffer long, difficult hikes, broiling heat, cold, wind, rattlesnakes—anything to see petroglyphs. Searching for these treasures is a pilgrimage for me and for them.

My affinity for Native American art, images on stone in particular, has manifested itself other ways. After a long hiatus as an artist, except for commercial work, I began to do my own artwork again in the early 1980s. Scores of the mixed-media sculpture pieces that came forth were distinctly shamanic in feeling. My primary materials were animal bones. I loved the beautiful forms and learned that many Indian tribes believed bones to be the seeds from which life is reborn.

What I enjoyed most was transforming one thing into another in subtle ways. A stark white sheep skull might become a torso, a whale rib an abstract, crescent moon–shaped human, a cow's pelvis part of an eerie garment, or a turtle shell a birthing woman. People found my work either darkly beautiful or unsettling. I found solace working late into the night respecting and invoking the spirits of the creatures whose bones I used. The bones found new life in my work, a kind of transubstantiation through my mind and hands. I felt like a conduit for archaic memories seeking light.

A woman who later became a friend and collaborator sought me out at one of my first solo exhibitions. She was nonplussed by the fact I'm so obviously Anglo. "What are you?" she stammered, trying to find a category to put me in. "What's your background? Where did you grow up? Are you a . . . Jungian?"

I had to admit I was a Jungian. By then I had spent many years reading Jung, recording and studying my dreams and living close to my psyche, which had become as real to me as a part of my body—a kind of invisible appendage neither mind or heart, muscle or bone. I journeyed in dreams to places akin to the spirit I have sometimes felt in rock art while trying to recover from the death of a loved one—realms of mystery and power, beauty beyond anything my conscious mind could imagine. Caves filled with turtles whose shells were covered with jewels, cathedrals that defy the laws of physics, little mothers made of clay uncovered at a desert shrine. Snakes and bears to tame. To me petroglyphs and dreams reflect the same terrain.

Katherine Wells

Two

It was March 1992. I sat in the back of the realtor's SUV while Lloyd, my partner, sat in front next to "Mrs. P." I felt weepy. Lloyd and I had been in New Mexico for five days searching for a piece of property. I wanted to go back home to California and forget the whole idea of moving. As we drove along I wondered why I was crying. Fatigue, I decided.

Later that day I wondered if it was a premonition of a dream come true. Years later I wondered if the tears were a premonition of another kind.

I had made half a dozen trips to New Mexico over a three or four year period, looking for property by myself or with Lloyd. While I had long been attracted to New Mexico, for me the concrete idea of moving was planted on a trip to Taos with my friend Diane in January 1984. We went to the Buffalo Dance at Taos Pueblo on the sixth of January, Epiphany.

I was enthralled by what looked and sounded like a herd of bison approaching as we stood in the bright sunlit plaza trimmed with snow. The eerie sound of ululation came from Pueblo women standing on rooftops above me as the dancing "buffalo" slowly moved toward us. Pendleton blankets in bright reds, blues, and turquoise worn by the women heightened the scene. The dance was the first of its kind I had ever been to. The whole experience was primal and reached into my psyche with every drumbeat.

I grew up a severely asthmatic child in Kansas City, Missouri. My father, when drunk, often talked about moving to Albuquerque where my health would be better. He had worked for Fred Harvey briefly and went on and on about that city's clear, dry air. I knew we would never move, but in my imagination New Mexico became a place where I could breathe easily. Summer nights, as my lungs struggled to inhale in Missouri's muggy climate, I tried to summon a different, lighter air.

New Mexico's austerely sculpted terrain, raw colors of earth, and profundity of sky captured me on my first visit to the state in the early 1960s. In California, Caracas, and Kauai I have been seduced, visually sated by nature's most sumptuous color. But New Mexico spoke the idiom of my soul.

In 1957 when I was twenty years old I left home to go to college. I considered going to the University of New Mexico. I chose the University of Wyoming only because tuition for out-of-state students was cheaper. Soon after I met Lloyd in 1991 he told me of his own travels in the state and his interest in retiring here. He liked the fact that many roads had not been paved, that New Mexico's history has not been entombed under sheets of asphalt. We both liked the fact that New Mexico has not become culturally homogenized to the degree that the rest of the United States has. Most of the state still has distinctive characteristics like the soft lines of adobe architecture, the aroma of roasting chile peppers in any small town in September, the sweet odor of piñon smoke in winter.

Lloyd and I both wanted to be outside of, but within easy driving distance of, Santa Fe so we would have access to cultural amenities and an art market where I hoped to show my work. For those reasons during our visit in 1992 we were still searching for the "perfect" place to live. Our property search had taken us as far south of Santa Fe as Galisteo and as far north as Taos.

Our hope was to find property with a house so we wouldn't have to start from scratch and build. We ruled out several pieces of raw land our Santa Fe realtor mentioned. Both Lloyd and I had requirements. I insisted on a view of the mountains. I saw my first peak in Colorado at nineteen and promised myself never to live out of the sight of mountains again. Lloyd refused to buy property on a straight street. He had been in the suburbs of Southern California too long.

We looked at everything from an elegant home near the Santa Fe Opera House to a fixer-upper in Los Luceros. Nothing suited us both. Lloyd called Mrs. P., an Española realtor, about a parcel of land we had seen near the village of El Rito that Lloyd thought looked interesting, even though the property had no house on it. She explained that we should not consider the lot because of title problems. She mentioned a couple of other parcels she could show that might interest us. We had not thought in terms of more than a few acres; both properties were large and cost more than seemed wise to spend on land alone, but reasonable on a per-acre basis. One, she said, had some petroglyphs. "Right," I thought, "probably a couple of little squiggles on a rock." I assumed that the government or Indian tribes owned all the petroglyphs. To please Lloyd I agreed to look at the two parcels the next morning.

Mrs. P. turned off the highway a few miles north of Española and headed toward a mesa. We crossed the Rio Grande and followed a road through a tiny village that was not on our map. We then turned off the pavement onto a dirt road going uphill. Mrs. P. asked Lloyd to help her unlock a cable gate while I tried to absorb a landscape strewn with giant, black basalt boulders. Large juniper trees dotted the hillsides. The day was warm, calm, and almost balmy. A sweatshirt was all I needed for comfort.

After a quarter of a mile Mrs. P. turned left onto a large, flat open area covered with native grasses, cholla, and prickly pear cactus. We got out of the vehicle and I looked up at the hill above us and saw the dark expanse of a boulder the size of a one-car garage. The face of the rock was covered with petroglyphs. The hair on the back of my neck stood up.

While I sprinted up the steep, rocky hillside, Mrs. P. began to unroll the plat map. My fatigue vanished. I reached the boulder gasping for breath, my heart banging for joy. I put my hand on the stone's sun-warmed surface. Before me were images of lightning-shaped snakes, a cloud terrace, a crescent moon, a four-pointed star, and a mysterious bird. All were beautifully pecked into the rich brown patina covering the mammoth stone.

I stared at the glyphs for a while, trying to take in the perfection of the moment. Then I turned around. The Rio Grande shimmered through bare cottonwoods along its banks below. Across the valley in the

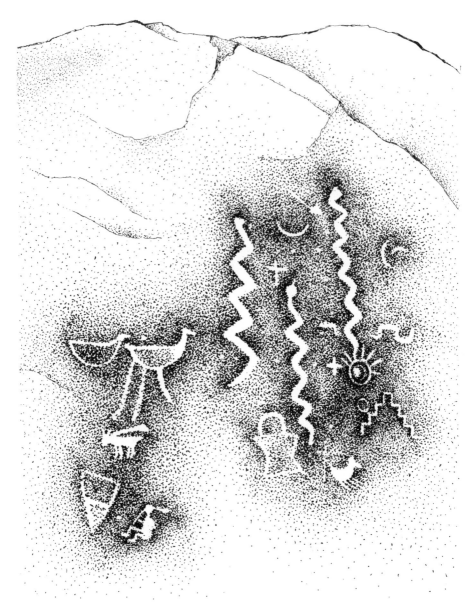

The Key Rock with images of lightning-like snakes, celestial
objects, animals, and a tiny flute player.

Katherine Wells

distance the snow-laden Sangre de Cristo Mountains stretched across the eastern horizon. This would be my view. I would live below this sacred stone and stare at the mountains. I would live in a tent if I had to, but here I would live. In the rapture of the moment I forgot about Lloyd. I was home.

I recovered my composure on the way back down the hill so as not to look too eager. Mrs. P. and Lloyd were poring over the map, pointing this way and that and discussing various aspects of the property.

The plat indicated that the parcel was 188 acres. The owner lived in northern California and had been on the property only a time or two in the thirty years he had owned the land. He was willing to divide the piece into two equal parcels. The property had been on the market for a couple of years and Mrs. P. thought the owner might come down on the price.

The idea of owning so much property seemed preposterous, yet appealing. Lloyd had sold his house in California and mine was on the market. We could probably swing the deal with enough money left over to build. We walked around for a few minutes trying to imagine the possibilities. Lloyd liked the place but was eager to see the other parcel Mrs. P. spoke glowingly about. I could not imagine anything having more appeal than where we stood, but I went along. On the way back to the paved road I spied a few other petroglyphs and vowed to lure Lloyd back later in the day without Mrs. P. so we could have a better look.

To reach the other parcel we drove a few miles past Abiquiu, turned onto Highway 96, and crossed the Abiquiu Dam. We were headed toward the tiny village of Coyote. Several miles later we were near the foot of the majestic Pedernal, made famous by the paintings of Georgia O'Keeffe.

Mrs. P. turned off the road in the direction of the Pedernal. We got out of the car and walked around a bit. Mrs. P. pointed out the boundaries of a beautiful one-hundred-acre parcel covered with soft grass.

The forested mass of the Pedernal lay in one direction. In the other was the deep blue water of the Abiquiu Reservoir surrounded by vast expanses of smooth vermillion rock. Breathtaking. Lloyd was smitten. I knew he was already thinking about the best site for a house, the best angle for views and solar gain.

I'm in trouble, I thought as I studied the look of delight on Lloyd's face, but I knew how I would make my stand. The property was almost fifty miles from the nearest grocery store, but my petroglyph heaven on Mesa Prieta was less than fifteen. A sense of aging had not hit me yet at fifty-five (Lloyd was sixty), but common sense dictated that we think long and hard about living so far off the beaten track. Lloyd had little interest in petroglyphs, but I hoped to convince him that the mesa property was a better choice for us both because of its proximity to Santa Fe. He was a romantic, but I would appeal to his practical side.

An hour later Mrs. P. dropped us off at our car. We thanked her and said we'd be in touch. After lunch at JoAnn's Restaurant in Española Lloyd and I headed back to the mesa and spent two hours walking the land I wanted to buy.

I lived on a postage-stamp parcel in California and the idea of owning 188 acres was utterly beyond my imagination. Since the terrain was almost completely steep up- and downhill we could get only a general sense of the parcel. There appeared to be half a dozen good building sites. Lloyd and I liked that there were so few, and the unbuildable acres made the price reasonable. I walked an open meadow and found a large, freshly dead owl whose feathers ruffled in the breeze. There was no evidence of how it met its end. I knelt by the creature for a bit and gently removed a feather.

I found several more petroglyphs and I began thinking there might be hundreds on the property. Near the cable gate next to the road was a glyph of a figure about two feet high. Its head was rayed like the sun. In the center of the face was a sphere. The being's arms were raised in what I think is a universal gesture of awe. Between its odd, two-toed, birdlike feet was a round form suggestive of an egg. Though the figure was an unusual glyph, it looked familiar. I couldn't imagine why. To me the being seemed to be an image of a deity, one that was eminently approachable, but full of mystery.

I fell instantly in love with the glyph. Because it was only a few feet from the edge of the dirt road, I marveled that the boulder had survived the road cutting process. I tried not to think about what had been lost to bulldozers. The fact that there were many other glyphs on either side of the road was evidence that some images were gone forever.

The rugged beauty of the terrain appealed to Lloyd, and he knew by then that he would have a tough sell getting me to sign on the line for a piece of property petroglyphless and fifty miles from town. "Hell, I'd give half my teeth to live in a place like this," he said, giving me a reassuring hug.

We headed back to California later that day. As we drove Lloyd and I talked about buying the property, the complications of building a house, and other issues. One thing I could not get over was the fact that having God knows how many petroglyphs on the property did not seem to add anything to the parcel's value as real estate. The per-acre price appeared to be consistent with other plots of land in the area without glyphs. As far as I could tell, the petroglyphs were free.

We turned west onto I-40 in Albuquerque as the last crimson streaks of sunset faded from the sky. Lloyd and I fell silent, each preoccupied with our own hopes, fears, reservations, and the myriad details to be dealt with and decisions to be made before New Mexico could become home. Before we just had a plan. Suddenly the plan was morphing into reality.

The newness of my relationship with Lloyd gave me pangs of ambivalence about the two of us buying property together. We had been together less than a year. Did we know each other well enough to be leaping hand in hand off such a high cliff?

Lloyd's mischievous blue eyes, sharp but subtle wit, unconventional intellect, and strong, capable hands attracted me. He wore his masculinity comfortably. Where I tended to be a planner he was spontaneous, sometimes impulsive.

His interests bespoke a complex mind. Lloyd loved *The New Yorker* (except when Tina Brown was editor) and listened endlessly to audiotapes of Ram Dass. All his life he had been obsessed with airplanes, boats, fishing, and the ocean. He didn't like Christmas, but annually watched *It's a Wonderful Life*. He adored cats. With breakfast he liked Bach, Kenny Rogers in the car. Lloyd's intense interest in politics was matched by contempt for politicians. He didn't care a bit about sports. Oh, yes, and he cut his own hair—with pinking shears.

One funny peculiar thing about Lloyd was an illusive tooth. I thought he had good-looking teeth when I first met him, but now and then for an instant one in the top front seemed to go missing. I thought the light was playing tricks. When my scrutiny became obvious he laughed and removed the tooth to show me. He had lost the incisor after an injury long ago.

Lloyd decided to try making his own false tooth because he couldn't afford a bridge at the time. He had an old boar-bristle hairbrush with an ivory colored plastic handle that was a good match for his teeth. He sawed a piece off and carved, filed, shaped, and sanded until he had a perfect replica of the lost tooth. By gluing a plastic tab on the back he got it to stay comfortably in place for hours at a time and no one was the wiser. Lloyd's dentist admired his handiwork.

The problem was that he lost the darling little denture once a year or so and had to make a new one. Lloyd liked to remove the tooth when no one was around. As he aged he began staining the new models with tea to match his aging teeth. By the time I met Lloyd the hairbrush handle was almost gone and he tended to lose the tooth more frequently. There were times we spent hours looking for the errant incisor in the leaves on a hiking trail, among the zillion tiny stones on a gravel road, and other impossible places. Lord knows how many times I washed the thing in his jeans pocket. I finally made Lloyd a small leather pouch he could wear around his neck to keep the treasure in when it wasn't in his mouth.

I thought about our short time together as we drove toward California that night, wondering if the whole moving venture would come to grief. Lloyd was born in Southern California and grew up there when the area was still largely rural. His family had raised chickens and kept a goat, grown fruit trees and a large garden. I wondered if I could become a "country girl" after living in urban areas all my life. A battle raged within me between fear on the one hand and the urge to forge ahead on the other. Risk seemed to be a large part of the equation.

How could I leave my friend Jean? We had taught school together, experienced many travel adventures together, owned a business together for almost ten years, shared mothering highs and woes. She was like a sister to me, as much family as my blood kin. I had no doubt that the friendship would endure, but I would miss being with her.

And what about my son, Tas? He was a junior at Harvey Mudd College and I saw little of him. He was in thrall of the brave new world of computers and spent his days and nights in front of a glowing terminal, oblivious to the rest of the world. Tas would go to graduate school and probably stay in California. A techie like his father, my ex-husband, his life would be where the high tech action was. He was already the owner of a burgeoning software business. My wunderkind, but I could not speak his language.

My relationship with Tas grieved me. He shared almost nothing of his life with his father or me. I knew Tas had to become his own person; I was proud of his intellectual prowess but pained by his unwillingness to communicate beyond a superficial level. I suspected my psychological absence during part of his childhood owing to problems of my own as one cause. I felt ambivalent about moving away because of him, but sensed that for the time being, nothing I could say would improve our relationship. I would have to be patient and hope.

On the other hand, many things pulled at me to get the hell out of California. The state had seduced me in 1961 when I moved thirty miles east of Los Angeles to Claremont, where Geza lived. The beach, the mountains, the desert, and the enticements of Los Angeles were all only an hour's drive away. The years passed, though, and the downside grated on me: traffic, smog, traffic, the Hollywoodization of everything, traffic, the desire for a simpler, calmer life in a different habitat, and traffic! I wondered if I might be suffering from "the grass is greener" syndrome. Was I romanticizing the beauty and culture of New Mexico?

Yep. I had been mulling the idea of making a move for several years but had doubts about doing it alone. Having a partner with a similar yen would make the wrench easier.

Back in California a major jolt of synchronicity reinforced my feeling that Fate was at work here. I kept puzzling over why the petroglyph of the figure with the sun head was so familiar. I owned only a few rock art books and none of them, as far as I remembered, focused on New Mexico, but I went through them searching for clues.

There was one book I had no memory of owning or buying titled *Suns and Serpents* by Gar and Maggy Packard. The authors self-published the volume in 1974. Only sixty pages long, the book was the work of petroglyph enthusiasts rather than scholars. Most of the images were from public petroglyph sites in New Mexico and Arizona. I was astonished to find a photo of the figure I was so taken by as well as a dozen or more images from Mesa Prieta that I had not seen. I was sure the authors had printed a few hundred copies at best. What were the odds I would have bought one somewhere years earlier and that one of its images would suddenly loom large in my life?

Lloyd and I continued to talk about the pros and cons of buying the parcel of land: whether or not New Mexico was really the place we wanted to be, what we could afford to offer, where we would live until a house was built, what kind of house to build, the best site for a house, whether to hire a contractor. Should Lloyd, who was a cement contractor and had worked at most of the building trades at one time or another, be the contractor? A million questions bumped around in our minds.

I lay wide-eyed many nights mentally shouting "yippee!" on the one hand and "now just a damn minute," on the other. What if the petroglyphs turned out to be an attractive nuisance like a swimming pool? Would we be liable? Did bad guys roam the mesa at night? What about robbery and rattlers? What if Lloyd and I split up? Was I burning too many bridges? My imagination went into overdrive.

Mrs. P. had given us a plat map, but there was other information we wanted before we made an offer. There was the fact that my house had not sold yet. My realtor had a potential buyer who changed her mind regularly. After a week or so we called Mrs. P. and reminded her to send real-estate "comps" that show the prices of properties recently sold so we could evaluate the price comparatively. A couple of weeks went by and we received nothing. Lloyd and I decided to go back to New Mexico and have some "face time" with Mrs. P.

We arrived on a day in early April and went to Mrs. P.'s office without calling first. She was at her desk near the front of the building. We told her we wanted to make an offer on the parcel. "I'm sorry," she said. "That property is sold."

"Both pieces?" I sputtered. She nodded yes. I'm sure my mouth hung open a mile. Mrs. P. smiled primly, thanked us for our interest, and said to let her know if she could do anything else for us.

Outside Lloyd and I stood by the car in a daze. "I don't believe her," I snarled. "The properties have been for sale for two or three years and suddenly there are two buyers?" We called Mr. W., a Santa Fe realtor we had also been working with who was a friend of a trusted friend. He didn't believe her either. We knew the property owner's name and the California town he lived in. Mr. W. suggested that we let him try to contact the owner to see if the land was indeed sold and, if not, to make an offer. Lloyd and I told him what we were willing to pay. He said to give him a few hours.

We drove to the property. Knots the size of cannonballs volleyed around in my stomach. I climbed the hill above where we had parked that first day and sat at the base of what Lloyd dubbed the "Key Rock" because of its prominence in the terrain. I was on the verge of tears. I could not bear the idea of ownership slipping away. In a few short weeks I had spun an elaborate fantasy about my new life on the mesa: studying the glyphs, living in the beautiful house Lloyd and I would build, cultivating serenity in the beauty that surrounded me. Burying my face in my hands I asked the "Mighty Something" to let me be the steward of this special place. The word "please" passed my lips over and over like a mantra.

I knew that in the real sense, the petroglyphs could not be mine. Such cultural treasures are not ownable in the usual sense of the word. They are a legacy from those who came before on this land and belong to us all. I surmised that the ones on this land must have some connection historically to nearby San Juan Pueblo. The best I could hope for was an opportunity to take care of the petroglyphs for a while, learn what I could, share with others who revere them, give access to the descendents of those who made the images. My instinct was almost maternal. Little did I know what I was asking for. I saw some spray-paint graffiti and assumed I would be protecting them from inebriated teenagers and other thoughtless souls.

Lloyd and I went to the nearest pay phone about 3:00 p.m. and called Mr. W. My hands shook as I dialed the numbers on the rotary phone. Mr. W. had spoken to the owner who had accepted our offer and reduced Mrs. P.'s commission to one thousand dollars. I was elated beyond words and kept jumping up and down in the parking area by the phone booth. Lloyd was happy, but more restrained. He smiled at me as though he were indulging a child. Our big adventure had just begun.

I learned a couple of years later that there actually was an offer made on half of the property a few days before we made ours. The seller had accepted the offer, but reneged because ours was for the whole piece. My feelings toward Mrs. P. softened.

Lloyd and I both felt we needed to live on our land for a year or more before building. We wanted to learn the weather patterns, understand the terrain, pick the best site for a house, and figure out how to minimize disturbing the land. It felt important to "impose" on the site as little as possible. We also needed to learn more about local building codes, figure out what style of house to build, get recommendations for builders and materials sources, and a thousand other details.

Lloyd and I had read an article in *Fine Homebuilding* magazine a couple of months earlier about a structure in Davis, California, that someone had constructed out of baled straw, then coated with stucco on the outside and gypsum plaster on the inside. The building was simple, elegant, and had an R-value of about fifty, which means very little heat loss in the winter or gain in the summer. We were instantly enamored of the idea. Building an ecologically sound house was important to both of us. We learned that pioneers built with straw in Nebraska over a hundred years ago because they lacked trees for frame houses. Some of those houses are still standing.

It was all heady stuff but did not address the issue of our "houselessness." My California realtor brought in an acceptable offer and I agreed to move out in sixty days. Lloyd and I thought about trying to rent a house near the property but decided instead to buy a small trailer and move onto the site. There was a well on the property—though we didn't know if it was a good one—and a power pole near where we parked the first day. Mrs. P. mentioned that the owner's brother had lived there in a trailer for a few years in the 1960s.

Our trailer could be home while we settled into the area and during the building process. Buying one in California that we could pull to New Mexico behind Lloyd's truck seemed sensible. We would pack it with clothes, linens, dishes, cookware, and other essentials. Furniture, artwork, tools, and other possessions would follow in a moving van and be placed in a storage unit until we were ready for them.

The search for a trailer began. We quickly found one thirty feet long made by the Silver Streak company that was much like an Airstream.

Though more than twenty years old, the Silver Streak had been well cared for and did not show much wear. The interior was thoughtfully designed. Not an inch wasted. The "Streak" felt snug and homey and would suit our needs well.

I had lived on a boat with much less space than the trailer for weeks at a time with my ex-husband and felt confident that I could adapt to life in the Streak. Lloyd teased me though. "Honey, it's here," he yelled one day in a fake Okie accent after checking the mailbox. I looked at him with a puzzled expression. "This month's issue of *Trailer Life*," he joked.

Some of my friends expressed concern about my ability to be content in a rural environment without the amenities I was accustomed to. Was I being naïve or unrealistic? Perhaps.

Bronwyn, one of Lloyd's two tall, beautiful, red-haired daughters, got married at sunset on the beach at Newport the night before we left California and headed toward New Mexico. She was a floral designer and her new husband an haute cuisine chef. The wedding was a fancy do, indeed, with lots of people I had never met. Lloyd in his tux was as handsome as if he had been rented with the suit.

We left for New Mexico the next morning at 6:00 a.m. even though we had not returned from the wedding until the wee hours. We hoped to beat the worst of the California desert heat. Lloyd and I had been going full throttle continuously in the weeks before the move. The frantic pace was especially hard on me. Lloyd's house had sold six months earlier than mine. He had already taken care of all of his stuff. I still had rugs, paint cans, boxes of tax records, and God knows what in addition to all the angst and baloney that go along with selling a house. I was pushing, pushing, pushing.

I drove my Dodge Colt Vista 4WD wagon and Lloyd his ancient, yellow, beat-up, behemoth of an International 4WD truck, pulling the tidy-looking Silver Streak. He had bought the truck at a Southern California Edison company surplus sale. The vehicle had neither heating nor cooling nor headliner nor door handles that could be operated by anything less than a four-hundred-pound gorilla. Beefy engine and tires big enough for a 747, it had.

A great New Mexico truck, Lloyd assured me, i.e., a real guy's truck. He was the first man in my experience who had a major passion for things on wheels. To me cars were just machines to take you from point A to point B. Lloyd found my attitude incomprehensible. "Ask me what kind of car I have," I said in one conversation about automobiles. He looked puzzled, but asked. "Blue," I replied. Our discussion ended with him just shaking his head. A couple of days later he said with excitement, as though a light bulb had just been switched on above his head, "I think I get it. To you a car is kind of like an appliance." The fact that I had no more emotional investment in my Dodge than I did in my Frigidaire was a major revelation to him.

The best Lloyd's truck could do with the trailer in tow was about fifty miles per hour and his gas mileage was down around ten miles per gallon. Lloyd carried a couple of jerry cans of fuel, but still we had to stop at every third gas station. Drafting in the Streak's wake, I was getting close to thirty-five miles per gallon in the Vista.

We moved with one pet, Lloyd's gray and white cat Dina, who had been left behind when one of his redheaded daughters went elsewhere for a job. Dina rode in the trailer. We stopped a couple of hours into the Mojave Desert to check on her. She was hiding in a tiny compartment. When we pulled her out she was panting and bedraggled. We cooled the cat off the best we could and put her on the floor on the passenger's side in my vehicle. She purred and the air-conditioner hummed as we crossed into Arizona.

That night we parked outside a friend's home in Flagstaff and slept in the Streak. After an excruciatingly long day with truck problems and the heat, I was even more done in than the night before. My neck was stiff and my back ached from an old injury. Lloyd could drive from here to the moon without tiring, but for me more than a couple of hours behind the wheel was stressful.

Three years earlier I had been diagnosed with an autoimmune disease called polymyalgia rheumatica. The condition causes muscle stiffness, pain, and fatigue. The symptoms had abated and I no longer had to take steroids, but my energy level was still low. In spite of my fatigue we got back on I-40 about six the next morning.

The never-ending line of big rigs blasting past our slow procession of truck, trailer, and car unnerved me. After quirky truck behavior, numerous fuel stops, and consoling rests for Dina, we pulled into Blake's Lotaburger in Española about 9:30 p.m. Lloyd was crabby because we had eaten only snacks all day. I was beyond crabby from fatigue, too much junkfood, and a ripping backache. I assumed Blake's would have chicken or fish sandwiches, but alas, only beef. I ate French fries. Lloyd proclaimed his burger to be the worst he had ever tasted.

I felt gritty and wanted to check into one of Española's mom-and-pop motels and enjoy a shower, a soft, clean bed, air-conditioning, and a night of oblivion, but Lloyd's compass was set. He wanted to forge ahead to the property.

"We're almost there," he pled. "Let's go." I got behind the wheel against my better judgment and made a mental note to stop giving in to him so easily. We parked off the pavement on the wide, dirt turnout where the road started uphill onto our land. My anxiety level was as high as Everest. Sleep would not come. Lloyd was out in thirty seconds. He was up at 6:00 a.m., bright-eyed and his usual irrepressibly cheery morning self. Why early risers and night owls so often have a mutual attraction will ever be a mystery.

"Come on, there's work to do," he said, shoving a can of juice at me. I got up, bumped my bleary way out the door, and went in search of a juniper to pee behind. A cholla cactus snagged me on the way back to the trailer. Lloyd heard me swear.

"Hey, I want a smile on that face, Kiddo," he chided.

"Go to hell," I yelled, slamming the Streak's aluminum door behind me. He opened it gingerly after a couple of minutes. "I'm exhausted," I bawled. I felt like I might bawl until Christmas. Finally he came in.

"Why didn't you tell me?" he sighed, stroking my hair. I wanted to strangle him. It was one of those moments between a man and a woman that never cease to amaze me. I had told him I was tired at least a dozen times in three days and gotten some kind of acknowledgment. I thought my plight had registered. Should have known better. Fatigue had battered the excitement out of me while adrenalin fueled Lloyd's full-speed-ahead mode. I slept another hour while Lloyd hiked up the road and figured out where he would set up the trailer.

He sited the Streak within a few yards of the power pole and about fifty feet downhill from the covered, subterranean well house. The view was perfect. When the Streak was leveled we sat down with cups of coffee and breakfast bars to catch our breath and take in the view.

Cumulous clouds were beginning to mound over the Sangres. The highest peaks were still graced with a bit of snow. The river now was lined with giant cottonwoods in full leaf, stretching upriver toward the canyon leading to Taos and south through the valley on its way to Texas and the Gulf of Mexico. A hawk loafed on a thermal overhead. The Key Rock stood with its face lit by the sun as it had for millennia of millennia. I loved the stillness and aura of timelessness surrounding me. This is what I had come for and what I would work to preserve. I squeezed Lloyd's hand. He winked and squeezed back.

After breakfast we went to work dealing with the less than ideal details of our new world. First, we needed to visit the title company office and sign the final papers on the land purchase so Lloyd and I could get the purchase recorded. Then came the more difficult tasks of arranging for the power to be hooked up and having a well pump installed so we would know if our water source was good and if there was enough of it. We had banked on the fact that there were a couple of other homes at the same elevation a mile or more away on the mesa that had good wells. We also had to arrange for phone service and figure out what to do for a toilet.

None of these tasks proved quick or easy. We had moved partly because of the attraction of a slower life-style, but found slower torturous when dealing with basics like power and water. If there had not been power already available on the property we probably would have gone off the grid, but we took the easy way and plugged in.

The people from the power company came within three days. Lloyd chilled some wine to celebrate having lights and refrigeration.

After ten days or so, I was beginning to think we would need an act of Congress to get a well pump or a phone line hooked up. Without a telephone (cell phone service was not available in the area then) it was hard to make anything happen. The nearest pay phone was at a Conoco station four miles away. We went there once or twice a day to make calls. The owners of the gas station were kind enough to fill our containers with fresh water until we had a functioning well.

Katherine Wells

Katherine Wells, Lloyd Dennis, and Ringo with the Silver Streak.
Photo by Jean Gillingwators.

The weather was hot—in the mid to high nineties most days. A small strip of our land bordered on the Rio Grande. We tried bathing in the cool river water. Privacy was not an issue because the cottonwoods and Russian olive trees provided a leafy screen. A picture I took of Lloyd smiling while bathing au naturel looked like a scene from Eden, complete with Adam washing his armpits.

In reality the area close to the river was a mosquito-ridden hell. Few of the infuriating creatures ventured up the hill where the trailer was, but on the river hungry hordes awaited our daily arrival. You could almost hear them smacking their tiny lips as we approached. I soon cried "uncle" and decided I would rather be dirty or make do using our borrowed water for spit baths than brave the swarming beasts on my backside—all sides—one more time.

The day the well pump installer finally came was one of high drama. We were relieved to learn that we had copious amounts of good-quality water. Seeing the sweet, clear liquid arc from the installer's hose on a hot afternoon felt like winning the lottery.

The trailer had a tolerable bathroom with a tiny tub/shower, vanity sink, and working toilet. Whether to use the toilet was the first issue to deal with. We weren't ready to install a septic tank and leach field because we weren't sure where the house would be. There were several possible locations. We considered the toilet solution many people choose with temporary trailer situations—build a "Forest Service" system—which means burying a fifty-five gallon drum in the ground under the toilet outlet and putting in some lime, but decided against it.

As a stopgap measure Lloyd carpentered together a seat over a pit that someone had dug long ago about forty yards from the Silver Streak. The commode featured a plastic bag to hold a roll of toilet paper and a shovel to be used for pitching a little dirt in as needed. We replaced the plastic bag with a watertight container a couple of days later when we had our first summer rain and soggy TP.

I had lived with an outhouse as a child and camped and backpacked most of my life. Using the Outhouse of the Great Outdoors was not an issue in summer. Except when it rained. Trudging off to the pit at night wearing my blue slicker and toting a red umbrella a couple of times during a downpour focused my mind on finding a more civilized solution of some kind!

The one sad note of the first month was Dina. She was not happy being confined to the trailer so we began to let her out for short periods. It seemed risky because she had known only the protection of enclosed backyards. Usually she stayed close to the trailer. One evening we could not find her. Lloyd fretted because we heard coyotes nearby. The mesa was their home ground. A California house cat would make as good a dinner as a hapless rabbit for these wild canines.

The next day Lloyd found a dead coyote down by the paved road. He buried the predator believing it had killed Dina. I watched him dig the grave in silence. He was bereft and angry with himself that he had brought Dina to a place where she was not able to survive.

Katherine Wells

Three

I was out petroglyph sleuthing for at least a short period each day. The luxury of prowling the rocks and finding more and more intriguing images on my own land was heady and humbling. I had an ever-stronger sense of the ancient people who made and used the glyphs. Were they looking over my shoulder laughing with glee? I felt welcomed and my resolve deepened to protect the images earlier inhabitants had left.

Every day I was more in awe of the images individually and collectively. I suffered acutely from a poverty of vocabulary. "Wow" and "good grief," "geez," and "omigod" served as inadequate but necessary utterances. Every day I revised my estimate of how many there might be and how important the site was, how crucial my budding stewardship might be. Lloyd agreed that the petroglyphs should be protected beyond our ownership, but our thoughts were amorphous. It was too soon to conjure a plan for the future.

I recognized how unique my experience was and felt blessed. Some days hiking around my domain I ruminated about how my father would have viewed my life. I had been born into a poor family at the tail end of the Great Depression. My father expected nothing of me except that I stay out of trouble, get married, and get out of the house. He denounced education, especially for girls. Sad to say, but I think he feared his children would be smarter than he was. In spite of uninspiring beginnings I worked my way through college, graduated Phi Beta Kappa, and won a Fulbright scholarship to Venezuela.

Life had smiled on me in many ways through some agency I little understood and here I was in a place, a circumstance, I could never have imagined. What fate, what funny karma, what dumb luck, what random winning ticket had I drawn?

I realized that another human had probably not seen some of the remote and less visible glyphs for hundreds of years. Glyphs are often obscured during part of the day because of the way light reflects on the surface of basalt. Older glyphs that have repatinated through interaction between the environment and organisms on the rock over thousands of years may be all but invisible in the best of light.

I concluded that there must be thousands of glyphs on our land alone and that I would have to examine every side of every rock in every light to see them all. Beyond our boundaries, I thought, there might be thousands more images.

I began to gather and read what I could find about the northern Rio Grande area and New Mexico, the Southwest, and the larger domain of world rock art. I learned that serious interest in rock art as a subject among archaeologists and scholars had only begun a decade or two earlier. Historically "Dirt Archaeologists," i.e., men, did not consider rock art worthy of study because it could only be dated relatively. Petroglyphs and pictographs were more suitable as a subject of inquiry for women or dilettantes.

I was flabbergasted. These images were an effort by humans from the past to communicate and record their experiences and mental processes. Why would anyone conclude that ruins or spear points or pots were more useful or deserving of study? Happily, that attitude has changed in the archaeological world.

Polly Schaafsma's *Rock Art in New Mexico*, published in an updated edition in 1992, was at the top of my list of books. In this text I found the rudiments I needed to know about the area's history, from the arrival of Paleo-Indians about ten thousand years ago to the present-day Native Americans who live here.

Katherine Wells

One of the site's most dramatic shield bearers holding a spear.

A few glyphs from the mesa were pictured in Schaafsma's book, but little specific information was given. Indeed, I discovered that not much information was available that focused on the mesa. A couple of years later someone loaned me a tiny book called *Selected Petroglyphs in Rio Arriba County* by Helen G. Blumenschein. Published in 1973 by Pruett Press in Boulder, Colorado, it consisted of a few pages of not very informative text and twenty-five black-and-white photographs of petroglyphs, most of them from our land.

Large eagle or thunderbird image.
Rio Grande Classic style.

From the various materials I read I learned that most of the petroglyphs surrounding me were created during what is known as the Pueblo IV period by the ancestors of present-day Tewa people in the period between approximately AD 1300 and AD 1600. Historians call them Anasazi or the more linguistically challenging Ancestral Puebloans. At that time large numbers of people moved into the area along the Rio Grande, perhaps from the Four Corners area. They may have come because of drought. Had some of those people camped where our trailer sat? Was the Key Rock a shrine? Had the early Tewa prayed for rain in front of the glyphs inscribed there? Were they as awed by the rosy glow of reflected sunlight on the Sangres as I was? Did they mind the mosquitoes while bathing in the river?

Among the most numerous and important petroglyph motifs are shields and shield bearers, sinuous snake or serpent images (many of which have two horns sprouting from their heads), human hand- and footprints, animal prints, spirals, concentric circles, four-pointed stars, human and animal figures and, most delightfully, many lively flute players. (The term Kokopelli is not used here because the original Kokopelli kachina of the Hopi people has a humped back and long snout, but carries no flute). The fact that there are more than a dozen whimsical flute players in animal form on the site was the ne plus ultra for me. More than in the rest of the country put together, judging from the literature. Why here? I wondered. What was their story? Did anybody know?

The early people made most glyphs by the process of pecking. Archaeologists believe shamans or medicine people, using small, sharp

Human hands that seem to be reaching out to the viewer from inside the rock.

rocks as chisels and larger rocks as hammers, created most. Some were incised or abraded. I puzzled frequently over the boulders the "artists" chose as "canvases." Why this one with bumps and cracks instead of that smooth one nearby?

I puzzled over the many unique nonrepresentational images looking for commonalities, lamenting that their meaning is lost forever. Hard and fast meanings, I read, can seldom be attributed to glyphs. A glyph that looks like a deer to me may have represented a hunting story, a clan symbol, a ceremony, a vision quest, or any number of other things to the person who etched it into the stone. Historians learned much from the early historic period and recent ethnography provides clues, but most petroglyphs will never be completely understood. While Columbus was sailing the ocean blue, perhaps a Tewa shaman carved an image here to mark the equinox of 1492.

When Columbus arrived in the West Indies, half a planet away from where he thought he was, large numbers of Pueblo people on the Rio Grande were building multistoried adobe structures with many

Shield-like object with probable frog attached and small human figure holding a giant spear.

Katherine Wells

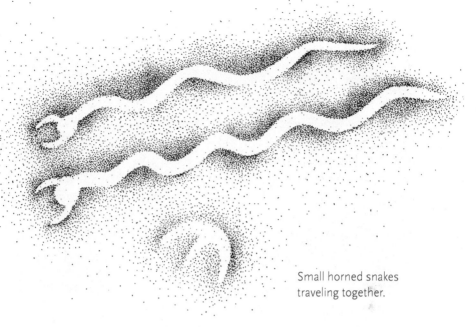

Small horned snakes
traveling together.

hundreds of rooms, cultivating maize, beans, squash, cotton, tobacco, and other crops, and designing elaborate water-control systems to irrigate their fields. They were trading with other groups as far away as the central valley of Mexico and the California coast, dancing as the seasons dictated, and making carefully decorated pots. Long before they laid eyes on the first of those who followed Columbus, germs from Europe arrived and decimated the Tewa and other Native American populations.

During my petroglyph forays, I found that there are also a large number of images pecked into the basalt by hunter-and-gatherer people who were in the region two to five thousand years ago, long before the Ancestral Puebloans. Some were etched when the Egyptian pyramids were being built, and others around the time Jesus was born.

Many of these glyphs are difficult to see. When I became aware of them I tried to develop a kind of X-ray vision to see them. I'd study a rock from different angles under different light conditions if I thought I saw something. Over millennia they have become repatinated to the point where they are the same color as the surrounding rock. Split or broken basalt boulders reveal that their interiors are pale in color.

Large boulder covered with heavily repatinated typical Archaic motifs.
Photo by Ekkehart Malotki.

Glyphs carved during the Archaic period began to appear more and more. Sometimes on my sojourns I carried a magnifying glass to study the images closely. Lady Sherlock on the job. People carved glyphs deeply during the Archaic period. For that reason their work is still visible in spite of patination and the ravages of time. Archaic images are intriguing because few are recognizable. Most are abstract, but certain motifs recur. Some resemble asterisks, centipedes, rakes, zigzags, squiggles, and what are called "one pole ladders"—vertical lines with a few perpendicular crossbars. Their antiquity and inscrutability make these glyphs all the more beguiling.

What on earth did these cryptic forms represent to those who created them? One theory among scholars is that the images are entoptic, produced within the eye by someone in an altered state resulting from drugs, fasting, sensory deprivation, or rhythmic movement such as ecstatic dance. Even pressing on one's eyeballs or being hit on the head

　　　　　　　　　　　　　　　　　　　　Katherine Wells

Historic period horse and rider, possibly a priest.
Photo by the author.

can produce entoptic images. We say we're "seeing stars." I repeatedly pressed on my eyes near a huge panel of Archaic images and saw lights and jagged amoeba-like forms. Maybe these entoptic images seemed magical to early people in the same way that comets, eclipses, and lightning did to early civilizations everywhere.

Along with the other petroglyphs, I found a significant number of Historic period images that were etched after the arrival of Vasquez de Coronado in 1540 and Don Juan de Oñate in 1598, but before 1950. Oñate established the first Spanish capital of New Mexico at Ohkay Owingeh Pueblo (formerly San Juan Pueblo) a few miles from Española more than twenty years before the Pilgrims' first bleak winter at Plymouth Rock. Among images from the Historic period are Christian crosses, horses, people on horseback, churches, European lions, names, dates, and initials. No one will ever know whether they were etched by Christianized Indians, mestizos or, perhaps, by Spaniards.

In many instances, Christian crosses were placed beside older glyphs, but never superimposed on them. Who would do that, and what were their motives? Would Christianized Indians or Spaniards carve them to negate the power of the glyph? If so, why not carve over them? Would the cross makers hope to borrow the earlier glyph's power?

In my late twenties I had flirted with the idea of going back to school and earning a degree in anthropology or archaeology. The endless mysteries I was now encountering made me regret that I had not.

The mesa appears to be archaeologically unique in that all three time periods, Archaic, Pueblo IV, and Historic, are well represented. Being used for target practice has marred a few glyphs and there are occasional instances of graffiti, but I was gratified to discover that for the most part local people and visitors have respected this bit of history.

There is evidence of frequent visitation over the years in the areas nearest the paved road. I worried because the steep slopes were being dangerously eroded. Sheep, then cows, had heavily overgrazed the whole mesa for more than two hundred years. Sharp hooves and teeth had decimated the vegetation. Excessive grazing and periodic droughts primed the site for a major loss of topsoil. In some cases the giant boulders used for petroglyphs are slowly being undermined from erosion caused by animals, rain, wind, and too many human footprints.

Because of the heat most of my petroglyph hikes took place in the early morning or in the evening. On the hottest days I felt like crawling under a rock. Since menopause began, I have poured sweat when others barely notice the heat. It has to do with brain chemicals and my "thermoneutral zone," the doc says. I think of it as a thermonuclear zone where I'm likely to explode. The temperature was no worse at the height of the summer than where I had grown up or where I lived in California, but I was spending so much more time out in the sun. Because of the nearly six-thousand-foot altitude, at least the nights were cool.

The only trees on the mesa are junipers, which, because of their shape and lack of height, provide little shade. The Silver Streak came with an awning furled into a metal casing that we cranked out. Age made the mechanism balky. The cloth had begun to shred from many years of sunlight.

One day Lloyd and I went shopping in Santa Fe and came home to find the awning in tatters. The wind had come up and whipped the fabric to pieces like a worn-out sail. I had never been in a tornado or a hurricane, but the shredded awning was an eye-opener, the first of many lessons about the ferocity of the wind in New Mexico. Strong winds are usually confined to springtime, but it can blow in wildly intense, short blasts any old time. I found an upholsterer who restored the awning to usability, but it was forever unretractable.

The monsoon began in mid-July. Afternoon or evening showers frequently cooled us off. The vivid colors of the sky and clouds building to crescendo over the Sangre de Cristos, the wild tines of lightning, the percussion of thunder deep in my bones, and the intense symphony of rain under vast tracts of firmament, were akin to a religious experience. Joy mixed with a tinge of fear. There was often an encore of double, and once or twice triple, rainbows arcing 180 degrees against deep cerulean skies. The most electric I had ever seen. I felt giddy in the face of such power and beauty.

I tried to imagine what life must have been like for the early people in the area at such times. They lived with much less protection from the elements than I enjoyed. How had they coped with deep snow in winter wearing only sandals or moccasins? How had they survived long years of drought when crops withered and there were few animals to hunt? How did they endure watching their children go malnourished or die of starvation? Burials and tree-ring dating that reveal periods of drought show that life was often harsh. What nature brought me was often stirring, sometimes difficult, but not a challenge to my survival. The first people on the land were unquestionably physically stronger than I but lacked the vast web of technological support that makes it possible for me to live here at this moment in time. I squirmed mentally following that line of thinking and the privilege it implied.

Sometimes Lloyd and I hiked cross-country to explore, looking for potsherds, spear points, and other evidence of early people on the mesa.

Because of cactus and rugged terrain we had to watch our steps. "I'll bet you the sandal maker was the richest guy in the village," Lloyd joked, referring to the mesa's early inhabitants on one excursion as he pulled prickly pear thorns out of his boot.

We often walked up our dirt road in the soft light of early morning. The dusty course continued about three miles and gained nearly a thousand feet in elevation before reaching the top of the mesa. Most of the time, we saw only one man, Paco, who lived a few miles south of us. He ran a couple of hundred cows on leased land.

Paco took truckloads of water to his cows each day. We enjoyed Paco's friendly wave as his ancient, green water truck crept up and down the road. One day when we were a couple of miles from home and the temperature neared one hundred degrees he offered us a ride. He had lived in a nearby village all his life and was a good source of information about weather and local history. Paco told us a little about D. J., a very odd young fellow who lived on the flat, treeless mesa top in a crude house without water, power, or a phone. He drove a battered pickup that needed a new muffler. He was the mesa top's only resident. Several years earlier D. J. and his father had built an underground house there.

Lloyd and I drove past D. J.'s abode once on a drive across the very rough dirt tracks that gridded the three-mile-wide expanse. Trash and car carcasses, car parts, and bones were strewn over an acre or two. A skinned, dead coyote hung on the fence post where one would enter his property. Good God, I thought, this guy is creepy.

As D. J. drove up and down the road almost daily in his severely dented truck, he never turned his head to examine the sight of our trailer, which had made an unannounced appearance, never returned our waves when he saw one of us. Then after a month or so, he stopped and introduced himself. We served iced tea and he sat with us under the awning for a few minutes. I felt awkward. I have never been good at meeting people and Lloyd was much less social than I. D. J. had us both beat by a mile. He avoided eye contact and did not smile. He offered almost nothing in response to our attempts at conversation, though what he did say was intelligent and articulate. I had an image of him in a noir Western directed by Sam Peckinpah.

Katherine Wells

D. J. seemed always to dress in black and he was filthy. I was repelled and fascinated. What did he do for water? Was he hostile or just shy? Did he have a job? Did he know anything about archaeology on the mesa? I asked questions that he answered with monosyllables or a vague nod of his head. After that day he waved on the road, but appeared to want no further contact.

The only other vehicles on the road were dump trucks. Mrs. P., the realtor, had mentioned that there was a local man named George Baker who hauled a few loads of rock, which he had stockpiled, off the mesa in the summer. Baker leased land from someone who lived elsewhere. The trucks had Valley Transit Mix signs on them. They were owned by Baker who, I learned, also owned a bank, a hardware store, many other businesses, and vast amounts of real estate in northern New Mexico. Perhaps a half a dozen sixteen-wheel trucks rumbled by daily.

I was alarmed when the creature came into view, a sinuous, two-horned vertical serpent called an Awanyu measuring twelve feet in length. The snake was pecked with great care into a coffee-colored megaboulder about fifty feet above a destroyed meadow at the head of an arroyo. Below on the ripped up meadow floor were mountainous piles of rocks with which George Baker filled his trucks. The locale had probably been a ceremonial site for native people long ago.

A bulldozer had wrenched the rocks out of the side of a hill rising from the meadow opposite the great serpent. Mining such a sacred site was anathema to me. I felt angry and sad seeing the majestic Awanyu in juxtaposition to the ravaged hillside and valley floor. Why here when there were other places with no petroglyphs nearby that could be mined? Here was one of the grandest petroglyphs in New Mexico. Now the image's context was being hauled away, apparently without thought. Archaeologists would never be able to learn the meaning inherent in the great snake's cultural and natural surroundings. Native Americans and those who appreciate what their ancestors left would never be able to look at this glorious glyph without sorrow. I felt the way I would if I had walked into a museum and found that someone had slashed a painting.

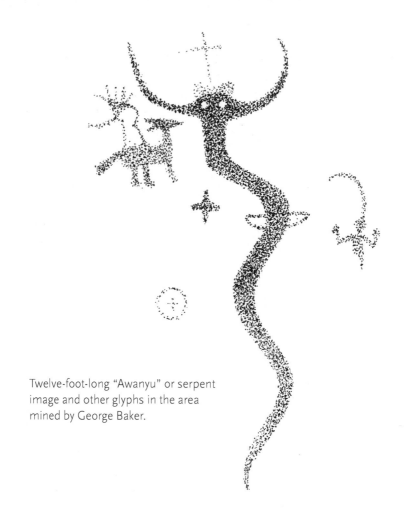

Twelve-foot-long "Awanyu" or serpent image and other glyphs in the area mined by George Baker.

Snakes are known to be water symbols. I thought the gargantuan glyph might have been a giant prayer for rain in a time of drought. I climbed around on the huge stockpiles of rock looking for more glyphs. The fact that I found none did not mean that there weren't some I couldn't see or some that had already been hauled away. The trucks stopped running after a few weeks, much to my relief.

Our nearest neighbors, Pete and Alicia Hughes, lived about a quarter mile to the south on the paved road running along the foot of the mesa.

On the other side of the road were fields and bosque, then the river. We stopped and introduced ourselves to the Hugheses after we first visited our property. Pete was the archetypal Western Man. An aging Gary Cooper: tall, quiet, no nonsense. He had worked for the Department of Game and Fish for many years and then as a hunting and fishing guide. He had half a dozen hounds in the yard that created a commotion when Lloyd and I drove up. Pete knew more about the mesa and the area than almost anybody else around. Alicia was a strong, energetic Hispanic woman who offered us homemade biscochitos and coffee.

Pete was patient with our newcomer questions. No, there weren't many rattlesnakes. Yes, he thought our well would be viable. After someone stole the well pump years back on the land we were planning to purchase he had covered the wellhead as protection from vandalism. No, there were no springs or other water sources on the mesa, although there had been in wetter times. Yes, he was very aware of the large number of petroglyphs though he had no idea how many there were. In the process of running a few head of cattle on the mesa years back he had seen hundreds of them. Pete and Alicia were protective of them and tried to discourage visitors who occasionally showed up at their door with questions.

I suspect Pete thought we were the greenest gringos he had seen in a long time, but he didn't pass judgment. After we had lived on the mesa a couple of years, I think he figured we might make it. In rural New Mexico, I found out, not everybody did. Many got chewed up and spit out. Some couldn't make a living. Others could not adjust to the ways of local culture.

I began to meet other people who lived in the vicinity as I continued to go out hiking. Some who were interested in rock art brought visiting friends or relatives. I met a few people walking the road or climbing the hillsides. I introduced myself as the new landowner and asked where they lived. Most were embarrassed to be caught trespassing, although there were no signs. They were happy to learn that someone interested in protecting the glyphs now owned the site. I reassured all the hikers that they were welcome to visit and asked them to let local people know what an important resource the petroglyphs were so they would feel protective of it.

After we had been living on the mesa for a few months, I ran into a big bear of a man. He was leading a half dozen people around, showing them an area densely populated with glyphs about ten minutes away from the trailer. I introduced myself and was greeted with great enthusiasm. The "bear" was Paul Williams, head Bureau of Land Management archaeologist in the Taos office. There was BLM land on the north end of the mesa that had many petroglyphs, Paul told me.

Paul was fully aware of the importance of my site and ecstatic that the land had been bought by a petroglyph buff. He had long worried that such a major rock art concentration had no steward. I, of course, was pleased to discover that someone who was knowledgeable and even had expertise about the glyphs held the site in such esteem. In my explorations I became very aware that all these images should be documented. I also understood that if I worked at it every day for the rest of my life I would never be able to complete the project by myself.

The visitors Paul brought wandered off in search of more images as we talked. He told me about the New Mexico Rock Art Field School, an arm of the Archaeological Society of New Mexico. The organization's volunteers had been recording petroglyph sites in New Mexico for more than a decade. Paul knew they would begin a new project the next summer and wondered if I would be willing to let them record the glyphs on my property. The Field School's leaders were aware of the site and interested in documenting the rock art.

The inadequate "wow" escaped my lips. The idea of having the glyphs recorded with the help of thirty trained volunteers was welcome indeed. Meeting Paul was the serendipitous beginning of a long collaboration.

My son Tas and his college roommate, Eric, came to visit in early August. One of them slept on the built-in bench or *banco* on the living-room end of the trailer and the other on the floor, which was spacious enough when we folded up the table. They brought Tas's dog, Ringo, a thirteen-year-old female beagle that had been living with Tas's father since my move. She had come to live with me. Ringo was in heaven and became my eager hiking companion. After spending her entire life in a small California yard, she now had almost unlimited terrain stocked with rabbits and other small creatures to harass. She never caught one, but the hound in her bloomed.

I took Tas and Eric on hikes to show them petroglyphs, drove them through a couple of pueblos, and gave them a tour of Bandelier National Monument, but mostly we stayed on the mesa. Tas and Eric were both very bright "geeks," but Eric, I learned, lacked common sense. The last day of their visit we were sitting outside after lunch and I noticed that Eric looked a bit strange. When I asked if he felt all right he nodded yes but said nothing. His face began to look cloudy and I asked again.

"I ate an ant," he said in a low, strained voice. I stared, not quite believing my ears. "I wanted to eat a grasshopper, but I couldn't catch one," he rasped on. I continued to watch the color drain from Eric's face. Near the trailer was a sizeable anthill with large red ants that I knew to be poisonous. One of the ants had bitten me on the leg the first week we were here. The bite raised a large, painful welt that lasted for ten days. Eric signaled that the ant had bitten him inside the throat. He appeared to be having an allergic reaction.

There was no time to ask why the hell he had eaten the insect or why he wanted to eat a grasshopper. I went into the trailer and got some Benadryl and a glass of water. Eric looked worse when I returned. He took the pill. I said I thought I should take him to the emergency room in Española. He shook his head no, but his breathing was becoming labored. Tas's eyes widened with incredulity.

"Get in the car," I barked. Tas put Eric in the front and climbed in the back. I drove as fast as I could. By the time we arrived at the hospital, Eric was breathing a little easier, but I checked him in and a doctor saw him within minutes. He gave him an injection of Benadryl. In ten minutes Eric was breathing normally. I looked at Tas, who rolled his eyes up as if to say, "I can't believe this is happening." The doctor wanted Eric to stay in the hospital for an hour.

I went to the pay phone to call Eric's mother for health insurance information. "He ate what?" she asked when I related the news. The conversation led me to believe that this was not the first time Eric had done something you wouldn't expect from a kid with a high IQ.

Tas thought the locale of my new home was interesting, but not to his taste. "No cell phone towers. No Internet," he moaned. "It's barbaric."

At twenty-one he couldn't understand that the lack of such amenities was part of what Lloyd and I liked about rural New Mexico.

Except for a few urban areas, the Land of Enchantment had not yet been "Californicated." Californians were, in fact, resented. They had been moving into the state in relatively large numbers for a few years and were driving up real-estate prices in Santa Fe. Fear of earthquakes and freeway fatigue had taken the glow off the Golden State. "Our" area was not yet affected by anti-California sentiment, but we changed the license plates on our vehicles shortly after moving.

Other California visitors that summer included my writer friend Kate Braverman, her husband Alan, and her daughter Gabrielle. Kate was strictly an LA girl. Her idea of roughing it was a suite at the Hilton. I took her on a trip to Baja California once where she suffered acutely from culture shock. She had no idea what real poverty was. It took several doses of the scotch I had brought along and a pricey tourist hotel to make her feel safe. Though an acclaimed poet and novelist, Kate's experience of the real world was a wee bit narrow.

Because we had no guest quarters, the trio camped out in a tent up the hill from the trailer near our property boundary. By nine the next morning no one had appeared, so I took a pot of coffee and some cups up the road. There stood Kate by their tent in matching lacy push-up bra and bikini panties, high-heeled mules, and sunglasses, as though she were at an exotic desert photo shoot. You can take the girl out of the city, but. . . . Even though she was light years out of her element, she endured the experience with considerable grace.

Katherine Wells

Four

Lloyd began to get testy and restless in August. Our agreement not to build a house until we had been in New Mexico a year started to rankle. Since he was young he had wanted to be an architect or an aeronautical engineer, but decisions and events denied him the necessary education.

He was always designing something. Lloyd had even designed, built, and flown his own airplane one time many years before I met him. The craft could not fly a second time because its maiden flight revealed a serious design problem, but he immediately began drawings and calculations for a second plane that he would build and fly someday.

Lloyd had a large draftsman's pad and he started sketching house designs. He was happy to draw and rethink and erase and change for hours. I didn't pay much attention since we were not planning to begin anything until the following summer. I thought he was just trying out ideas. Besides, I was busy hunting for more petroglyph treasures.

I underestimated Lloyd's need to be busy and using his hands. His frustration came to a boil one evening. "What did we buy all this land and move here for if you won't let me build anything?" he snapped. My eyebrows rose. Lloyd was gentle and mild-mannered 99 percent of the time, but I had learned by then to pay attention when the other 1 percent showed up. I did not remind him of our one-year agreement. He's got to have a project, I thought.

We talked about the possibilities. He agreed it was still premature to start serious house plans, but I would need a studio, so why not start thinking about that? Something simple. I couldn't come up with any good reason not to.

Lloyd became more and more enamored of the idea of building with straw bales, which also appealed to me because the concept was environmentally sound and we liked the idea of being latter-day pioneers. We knew there were a few such structures in New Mexico, but we didn't know where they were. From what little Lloyd and I had read, working with straw seemed to be a low-tech and forgiving process.

He eagerly set to work on drawings, and in a couple of days he had the basis of a plan. The building was a long, rectangular Pueblo Style design. The roof appeared to be flat but would slope just enough to drain. We would need long vigas to span the building's twenty-foot depth. There would be large windows in the front for solar gain and smaller ones in the back. Half of the space would be my studio and the other half a garage or workshop space. Lloyd wanted to build the studio facing the view and a bit closer to the dirt road than where the trailer sat so there would be plenty of room in the trailer's spot for a house if we decided to build there.

The first big problem was learning where to find good-quality straw bales. We would need about five hundred. We turned to the San Luis Valley in southern Colorado where wheat is a major crop. Nobody there had ever heard of building a real structure out of straw. "You're going to do what?" people asked. References to the three little pigs became a constant in our lives. At first Albert, the man we bought bales from, thought we were just another pair of nutty Californians, but after talking to Lloyd for a while, he began to understand the virtues of building with straw, especially in a cold climate. Albert was thinking about a new barn for his cows and asked us to send him some pictures of the finished studio.

In most straw-bale construction people stack the bales in staggered courses like giant bricks and pin them together with long pieces of rebar. Wooden posts provide roof support. Lloyd agreed that such a plan would no doubt be adequate, but he wanted to be sure the structure was extra strong. He devised a system in which he would drill a four-inch hole in each bale so that it would fit over a piece of four-inch PVC pipe. The pipes would extend from the foundation to the ceiling and be filled with rebar-reinforced concrete. They would also connect with the concrete bond beam when the cement was poured into the forms. The concept was overkill, but Lloyd liked the idea that in the end one could probably drive a truck into the building and damage only the truck.

We hired Manuel, a young man Lloyd had met in a hardware store in Española, and some of his brothers. The building process went smoothly in the early stages. Leveling the site, digging the trenches for plumbing, electricity, a phone line, and footings, putting the utilities in place, and having the footings poured all went well. There were many steps and details to attend to. I felt confident with Lloyd in charge. He was calm, methodical, and perfectionistic, a trait I would alternately appreciate and loathe over the next few years.

The studio was my first experience at building anything more complicated than a cardboard dollhouse. I was astonished at how many steps there were, how many decisions and problems, large and small, had to be dealt with every day, often under pressure. Building, I thought, was a little like swimming or sex: unless you have had the experience, it is hard to imagine.

As the procurement person, I was often sent to hardware stores in search of some item I knew nothing about—lag screws or bushings, valve reducers or adaptors, floats, flashing, gray board. More than once I swore when I returned with the wrong thing. Even though I took meticulous written descriptions and drawings, something often got lost in translation at the hardware store.

I learned that there are a dazzling variety of nails in the world. Sixpenny nails, tenpenny nails, roofing nails, finishing nails, duplex nails. Ditto screws. I learned about the weights of hammers, the properties of concrete, how to make a small straw bale, a "flake," from a large one. Arcane knowledge I never believed I would need.

I spent a lot of my time driving to Santa Fe or Española for materials, always racing to keep a step ahead so the process wouldn't slow down. Half the time I couldn't find what I was sent to buy. I hated the pressure and sometimes beat on the steering wheel and screamed, "I hate this," and occasional obscenities as I drove, but we needed to have the roof put on before the first snow.

I also did what I could as part of the work crew, mainly keeping things organized and tidy. Lloyd insisted on keeping a clean work site, which became an endless job once we started drilling bales and building the walls. Straw invaded the trailer, the gullies and crannies of our clothes, hair, eyes, mouths, and vehicles. I had to try to avoid the dust from the bales because of asthma. Once as a teenager I had a four-alarm attack on a hayride. I desperately tried to breathe and simultaneously keep the other kids, especially a boy I was trying to impress, from knowing I was ill. In my warped fifteen-year-old thinking my peers might see an asthma attack as embarrassing, humiliating, and weak.

Another of my jobs was crew welfare. This entailed providing snacks and drinks, hearing about girlfriend and money problems, providing rides when someone's vehicle broke down, and generally tending to whatever came up. The fact that I could speak Spanish—though mine was textbook stuff, very different from the dialect of northern New Mexico—gave me good standing among the crew. The guys thought it odd for a woman to be working on a construction job and sometimes called me "Patrona." I felt awkward among the López brothers because my life experience was radically different from theirs.

Hanging out with the crew was the beginning of my education about the social problems that have long plagued northern New Mexico's primarily Hispanic population: unemployment, drug and alcohol abuse, a deficient educational system, crime, and domestic violence.

Until World War II, northern New Mexico was isolated from mainstream American culture. The Catholic Church was the dominant social power and the population lived on a subsistence economic base. Farming and livestock provided for a family's needs. Few families were part of the cash economy. Education took a backseat when children were needed at home to help with planting, harvesting, or the care of younger siblings.

World War II brought abrupt change. Many of the region's young men went off to war and returned with a larger worldview. Others found low-level jobs at nearby Los Alamos National Laboratory where the atomic bomb was being built. The effects on an insular, church- and family-oriented population were broad. The young no longer wanted to

Katherine Wells

work the fields or tend livestock, but few had the skills or education to compete in the new economy. The bonds of family, religion, and language frayed. Alcoholism and then drug abuse invaded communities like a marauding army. To this day alcohol and drug addiction take captive after captive with far too little organized resistance.

The López family, we learned, had twenty children. That any woman in our country would allow herself to become pregnant twenty times at the end of the twentieth century shocked me, though I said nothing. One of the brothers said with a laugh that their parents had not had a TV. Later he said that he wanted to have twenty kids, too. "Why?" I asked, trying to disguise my disbelief.

"My parents did it," he shrugged. I puzzled over how I could tactfully broach the subjects of educating children and the problem of overpopulation.

Among the brothers, only Manuel had regular, full-time employment. Many of the kids still lived at home and survived on odd jobs or welfare. We hired Gerald, Eddie, Pablo, and their friend, Carlos, who were all in their twenties during much of the construction period. Just one had finished high school. We would never have a labor shortage. The guys liked working with Lloyd. The idea of building with straw was bizarre to them. They couldn't fathom the concept until the walls went up.

My petroglyph searches went on. Someone I had met from across the river told me about what she called the "big upside-down person," about a mile and a half toward the top of the mesa. I began to search for the glyph with Ringo at my side and finally located it overlooking a high meadow of arresting beauty. Wow! Double Wow. He (I assumed "he" because most petroglyph human figures are thought to be male) is life-sized and upside down on a huge, elegant, eggplant-colored boulder. Parts of the body are solidly filled in, others partially so. The hands and feet are carefully and accurately rendered. There is what I think to be a halo of horns surrounding the head, and what I interpret as feathers project from the top. The face has small eyes and a rectangular mouth.

The image is the most powerful and important human representation

Magnificent life-sized upside-down horned human
figure on land purchased by George Baker.

46   Katherine Wells

I have seen on the mesa and, I think, surely one of the most significant in northern New Mexico. Several archaeologists who have seen the figure agree. Visitors and local people who had seen the glyph later told me they thought the being represented an alien who might have arrived in a spacecraft that landed nearby. I suppose this was because "he" appeared to be falling from the sky.

To me the figure clearly fit within the Pueblo IV time frame because of its style and patination. I had seen a few smaller upside-down figures on my site. Something I read conjectured that the position might mean death—actual or symbolic, as in a shaman's trance. My hunch was that he represented a very important person, a shaman, perhaps, who died or experienced symbolic death in an extraordinary spirit journey. I don't know anyone who has seen the glyph who did not experience a sense of awe and the unknowable in its presence. I sat on the ground happily wordless.

Being alone with the upside-down being in its silent, undisturbed landscape felt like the rarest kind of privilege, better than meeting presidents or queens or seeing the faux Lascaux with tourist hordes. I sat in the morning shade of a nearby juniper wishing I could better span the gap between the shamanic mind and my own meager imaginings.

I have a sense of the spiritual, have plumbed the realms of dream and psyche and know through personal experience that the unconscious is real and plays a powerful role in individual and collective lives. I can easily see the commonalities of myth in the river of history and understand the grip of symbols. But I am still Science's child, deprived of belief in virgin birth or magical flight, agog at Hubble's views of the universe and the cosmos under a microscope. Who is to say which is richer? Perhaps I love rock art because it is a door, a tiny glimpse into an illuminating world.

A newer, Historic-era image appears on a large boulder a few feet from the upside-down being. The figure is a human about three feet high sporting a hat and skirt with buttons down the front of its garment. I wonder if the glyph represented a Catholic priest, as its clothing appears consonant with an early friar's garb. Juxtaposed with the upside-down figure, that makes sense. A minion of the new religion boldly etched beside the old.

When Lloyd and I asked who owned the vast stretches of the mesa beyond our boundary, Mrs. P. had mentioned the widow of a man who lived in Washington State. She owned several thousand acres on the mesa that were part of a land speculation deal in the 1960s. Paco, the cattleman, told us George Baker leased land from the widow for his rock hauling business. I wondered if she had any clue what important archaeological treasures populated her property. The mesa had been the subject of little archaeological study, but obviously is a major area of importance that deserves investigation and protection. There were no "Private Property" or "No Trespassing" signs. Local people had apparently always freely hiked the mesa.

One of the curious things about petroglyphs on the mesa was what images were missing. Deer, elk, snakes, birds, dogs, lizards, foxes, dragonflies, coyotes, turtles, and other common fauna were represented. However, I thought it odd that I found no images of rabbits or fish even though jackrabbits popped up around me frequently as I hiked and fish thrived in the river.

I later read that a tale about Tewa ancestors falling into the river and becoming fish deterred the people from using them as a food source. But their ancestors would have needed the protein. And what about rabbits? I knew they were on their ancestors' menu. Why weren't they a subject of glyphs? All I can imagine is that fish and rabbits lacked sufficient magical or symbolic "charge." Being readily available for dinner did not seem to make an animal a desirable subject for a petroglyph.

I made another important discovery about a twenty-minute hike from the trailer. On a bluff above the public road and within spitting distance of the river I found a nine-foot-high boulder with weathered petroglyphs and lichen on all sides. I counted one hundred cupules, or cup-shaped forms, ground into the top of the stone.

Cupules made by ancient people have been found worldwide. While they are not images and are thus not petroglyphs per se, they are often found with rock art. The ones on what I came to call Cupule Rock vary in size from something you could place a golf ball in to larger ones that would hold a Texas grapefruit. Channels or grooves connect many. Judging by the patination, they are among the oldest human expressions on the mesa. Even though I knew I was not supposed to touch the forms,

I traced their cool, smooth edges with my fingers. I felt energized by this tactile connection with humans from long ago.

Most researchers believe cupules signify fertility or weather control. Some say that the material ground out of the stone may have been used ritually. With its proximity to the river and within the context of many other glyphs, Cupule Rock seems clearly to have religious importance. I climbed on top of it with difficulty. A perfect meditation spot. Sun, water, sky, stone: the presence of something holy. There are cupules here and there all over the area, but not massed together in large numbers as on Cupule Rock.

As Ringo and I walked back to the trailer that day, I thought about a recent note from a friend in California. Wasn't I afraid hiking around by myself, she asked? Weren't there snakes? What if I fell?

Her questions brought home the jarring contrast between urban California, where humans have shaped everything, and the terrain around me. Most of what I could see had been little altered by my species. This was one of the things I loved—vast stretches of open land, a place to stretch my psyche, invite my imagination to forage in the clear air and peerless light.

I was cautious, but not fearful when I hiked alone. I watched carefully where I put my hands and feet when climbing among boulders. So far I had seen nothing more frightening than a three-foot gopher snake that I knew to be nonvenomous and inclined toward rodents for its diet.

Cactus is the real hazard. A moment of inattention and you can spend a half an hour pulling spines out of your clothes and flesh. Prickly pear lies in wait to assault your feet. Cholla behave as though your limbs and theirs are the component parts of Velcro. "They want to go with you," as writer Ellen Meloy observed. Tweezers became essential equipment in my backpack.

Perhaps curiosity and the thrill of the chase kept fear at bay. There was always another boulder luring me. I would swear in court that they called to me from a distance. "Great glyph over here. Come on," they would say. I always answered.

I mused on the Key Rock one afternoon, feeling warmth from the boulder radiate up through my body. I surveyed my Kingdom of Stone, dark gifts from the cosmos strewn artfully around the hilly terrain like so many sentinels: a silent, companionable population. Mother Nature's sculpture; my private sculpture park.

My passion for large rocks was not new. In California I had three of the largest rocks I could afford to have moved from a local quarry placed in my yard when I relandscaped. Diamonds don't interest me, but the giant boulders around me are like one-hundred-ton jewels, great chunks of psychic money. They made me feel rich in the way I once had standing among my small grove of fruit trees in California.

As a visual person I love the aesthetic perks of trees, flowers, water, sky. But rock has weight, resonance, gravitas. I love the sound of "stone," the sound of "rock," as words. "Stone" echoes, soothes, supports. "Rock" stops, holds. Both relay a solid kind of poetry. "The hills rock-ribbed and ancient as the sun," as William Cullen Bryant said.

Perhaps I'm drawn to stone for the same reason I love bare bones: shape, solidity, essence. Something ultimate. Something about my own rockness, stubbornness that has helped me survive. Stone strategy. The illusion of being a permanent feature of the landscape even as I erode and the rocks transmigrate atom by atom, quark by quark in the vast maw of geologic time.

How can I explain stone rapture, my visual and tactile attraction to monoliths? Here an elegant roundness like a hip, there a Euclidean angle. Veins of volcanic bubbles, elegant smooth swatches implying eons of flowing water. Colors of coffee and cinnamon; russet patches denoting iron. Rocks festooned on their northern and western faces with bouquets of lichen in many hues. I was absorbing the land stone by stone.

At the post office on a bright day in September I picked up a catalogue listing adult education classes being offered by the University of New Mexico at Los Alamos. Among them was a weekend class about rock art in northern New Mexico. There would be a Friday evening lecture followed by field trips on Saturday and Sunday. Great, I thought, a chance to learn more about glyphs and see other sites. I enrolled.

Katherine Wells

There were ten or twelve people in the class, most of whom had very little knowledge of rock art. The teacher, Mark Thompson, a freelance archaeologist, began to describe the sites we would be visiting. I quickly realized that Saturday's destination was my property. During the break I introduced myself to Mark as the site's new owner. He was a little embarrassed, but I assured him that groups such as the class were welcome to visit.

The studio walls were up by late September. Lloyd and I were both pleased with the rate of progress, even feeling a little smug. A fiendish wind came up late one afternoon just after the crew left. We went into the trailer to get away from the assault of flying straw.

We heard an odd noise while eating sweet, crunchy apples from a local orchard, a muffled "whump." We dashed out and found the whole back wall of the studio leaning in at a thirty-degree angle. A monster gust had whacked the carefully stacked bales. Lloyd labored until dark to get them pushed back into place and stabilized. He got into high gear preparing for the bond beam and concrete posts to be poured after that.

Word had spread around the neighborhood about our straw-bale project. Now and then someone would drive up the road to have a look. All were curious and some were leery. One old-timer sat on a bale and quietly watched the proceedings for about an hour. "That'll never work," he pronounced finally. He left shaking his head.

Lloyd had ordered extra straw bales for other projects. One was to build a temporary shed on one wall of the trailer to house a composting toilet. We had gone to an environmental design show in Los Angeles in the spring where we saw two or three kinds of toilets. One incinerated the waste with electricity. "Fried," Lloyd said. We rejected that because the contraption was expensive to operate, depended on the power grid, and was too complicated. Another was designed to use peat moss and bacteria to break down waste. On paper the concept sounded great.

Though the toilet cost more than a round-trip ticket to Moorea, I ordered one for use while we lived in the trailer with the intention of designing it into the house. In a couple of days Lloyd got the shed up and ready for use. We installed the commode according to the voluminous instructions sent by the manufacturer. Lloyd built a platform to keep the device off the ground. Our privy truly was a "throne."

We went through all the required steps to get the bacterial action to begin breaking down the waste and hoped for the best. Optimally, the compost drawer underneath would only have to be emptied every few months. I began to loathe the thing within a few weeks. The drawer had to be emptied much more frequently than stated in the owner's manual. Waste broke down to clumps of stuff that, fortunately, had little smell, but definitely seemed manure related. I took on the task of drawer emptying with scant cheer. "Shit," I muttered as a refrain on each occasion.

Another annoying problem with the toilet was the peat moss that had to be added with each contribution of solid waste. Since I had only worked with peat moss out of doors I failed to grasp how much fugitive material escapes. With every scoop, particles of peat moss wafted about. The dust was not a problem in the shed, but I did not look forward to having flurries of peat moss wafting around my house.

We also used extra straw bales to build a doghouse for Ringo. Adjacent to the shed Lloyd made a doggie domain completely protected from the weather. Then he placed bales two-high around the entire outside of the trailer in order to minimize the amount of cold air underneath when winter came. We knew the chill would migrate up through the aluminum shell as though the Streak were an oversized beer can.

The first week of October concrete flowed into the posts hidden in the straw and the wood-framed bond beam that rested on top of the stacked bales forming the studio walls. The second week our vigas arrived. Vigas are round, peeled, straight-as-an-arrow fir trees used as beams to support the roof. We had to hire a crane to hoist them into place. As is typical of Pueblo Style, the vigas protrude from the building's front and back and are exposed inside the structure.

Now we were ready to begin the roof. The work proceeded at a frantic pace. In a matter of a few days, pine decking covered the entire top of the building and was in turn covered with black roofing paper and a sheet of heavy plastic. Come rain or snow we didn't have to worry about wet bales any more.

Lloyd began the parapet next. Here, as with his idea to have concrete posts running up through the bales, he made an original contribution to the art of straw-bale building. By code, straw could not be used above the roof level. Lloyd decided to build the parapet using "pumicecrete," a combination of pea-sized pumice mixed with cement. The material had the advantage of being lightweight, strong, and shapable.

October was painfully beautiful. The vivid yellow cottonwoods along the river against a profoundly blue sky made every moment feel ethereal. For me fall is an altered state, serene and surreal. I wanted to hold my breath as though I could make the color last. Sometimes going about my chores or hiking the mesa I would look toward trees, mountain, sky and stop in mid-stride, mesmerized by color and light, trying to memorize the moment.

One afternoon I climbed halfway down the hillside below the trailer to where I had seen a flat boulder about eight feet across. There I found six smooth grinding slicks and a few petroglyphs. I absorbed the stone's warmth as I imagined Ancestral Puebloan women grinding maize on that spot. Women with long black hair pulled back, bangs shading their faces, matrons wearing simple woolen garments and deerskin moccasins, gray-haired women elders napping. I conjured them talking about the beauty of October's trees, the early snow on the mountains, gossiping as their children harassed chipmunks, sharing confidences and jokes about men.

My reverie suddenly made me hungry for female companionship. I was weary of the masculine energy that surrounded me day in and day out. All the macho body language men speak as they jostle together in physical work, their camaraderie. The spirit of those long-ago women who had ground the rock I sat on buoyed me, but I missed Jean and my other women friends. In the novelty of my new life I had thought little about what I had left behind. I had heard about a women's group in the area that met monthly for potlucks and poetry, music, and other activities. I resolved to investigate.

Autumn's cool days and nights were a balm after summer's heat. We felt sure we could insulate the studio roof and get the roofer scheduled

The studio, showing a straw-bale wall half covered by the first coat of mud plaster. Photo by the author.

before snow fell. New Mexico is noted for mild winters; with just a little luck. . . . Alas, winter came early.

A few days before Halloween we awoke to bright sun and three or four inches of snow glistening outside the trailer. I spent a couple of hours that morning sweeping the quickly melting slush off the roof of the studio with a broom. I had the same unhappy job twice more before the roofer finally came.

There were still many jobs for the crew to attend to: filling the space between the vigas with straw bale flakes, capping the back viga ends with sheet metal, building canales to drain the roof. One of the most labor-intensive tasks was "sewing" chicken wire to all the walls inside and out. To accomplish this, Lloyd made two twenty-four-inch-long needles out of one-eighth-inch metal rods. They were threaded with bright orange polypropylene bailing twine. One worker would be inside and the other outside sewing back and forth through the bales. This created a surface that would help the plaster adhere to the straw.

Katherine Wells

My petroglyph peregrinations continued as the studio-building project went on. I took advantage of the time whenever Lloyd didn't need me. Of all the motifs found in rock art on our land the one that charmed me most was that of flute players. They resonate with life and humor.

Try to look at one and not feel happy. Flute players are just up. They make you feel up. But their music gets down—jazz, bluegrass, reggae, in addition to soulful Native American melodies. It is difficult not to project onto them. This one's rapt by his own sweet etudes drowning the sound of a rumbling truck and dogs baying. That one's grandly phallic, piping high proud notes, knowing he could service ladies by the thousands. Another summons clouds, makes sounds like rain bathing corn.

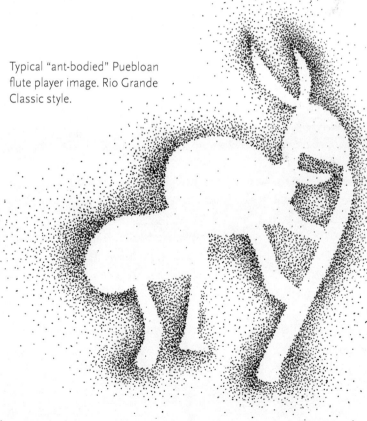

Typical "ant-bodied" Puebloan flute player image. Rio Grande Classic style.

Flute players abound on the site. Most appear as humans who are humpbacked or are carrying some type of sack or basket on their backs. The hump may represent a physical deformity such as Pott's disease, a form of tuberculosis that causes extreme curvature of the back. Sometimes the form is clearly a pack.

Nearly all of them have feathers or antennae sprouting from their heads. Many are extravagantly phallic. Several on my site have humpbacked, human-shaped bodies in a sitting position with long, gracefully curving tails. Others have ant-like bodies with tiny waists. Four are quadrupeds with long tails and ears. Coyotes? Mountain lions? No one will ever know with certainty.

One of the quadrupeds is high art. The artist knew how to make an animal image seem alive with his expert draftsmanship. The arc of the creature's tail, the attitude of its arms, the angle of his head, all bespeak an impressive sense of line. Some artists were able to make an image sing. Others had little sense of line, form, or the use of space. However,

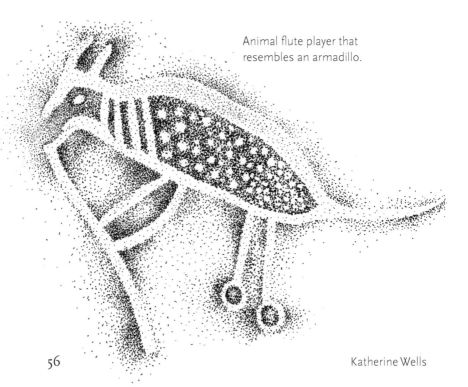

Animal flute player that resembles an armadillo.

Katherine Wells

Animal flute player with horned anthropomorph.

such considerations were not an issue since they were not making "art" as we understand the concept.

The most peculiar flute player looks like an armadillo in spite of the fact that armadillos are not native to the area. Perhaps a trader brought one here long ago from what is now Texas. Maybe a group of Tewa traveling south encountered one. Even Native Americans tell me the creature looks like an armadillo. The glyph is unique as far as I know.

Literature asserts that flute players had various roles in Pueblo culture. They represented fertility, were bringers of rain, seeds, or babies. They pursued maidens, melted snow, and stood as clan symbols, tricksters, traders, shamans, or magicians across the Southwest—beguiling creatures from the spiritual and supernatural world. I had enormous fun finding and photographing them, trying to divine their stories. I sat by my favorites listening, feeling that if I tuned in to the right wavelength, their songs might actually echo across the centuries.

I can't protect the flute player from its erroneous designation as "Kokopelli" in mainstream America. I sometimes think I am going to scream if I see one more transmogrification of the figure. Wal-Mart and thousands of other retailers in New Mexico sell garish images of flute players on cups, ashtrays, bookmarks, key chains, T-shirts, dish towels, potholders, jewelry, and any number of other objects. Ditto Arizona, Utah, and other western states. Most of these items are made in China. You can probably find a flute player image in Timbuktu by now.

The image has been co-opted for businesses as diverse as real-estate brokers and restaurants, even insurance agencies. I don't know whether I am more ticked off by the mindlessness of this massive cultural appropriation or the truly bad taste with which the flute player is, for the most part, appropriated. But bad taste or not, it's a testament to the flute player's charm.

As winter set in, life in the trailer changed in ways I had not bargained for: we had three ten-gallon propane tanks, which had to be hauled to town and refilled about once a week; the composting toilet composted very sluggishly; and water froze in our pipes.

One of the rudest surprises came that first time snow fell. I got up before daylight to go outside and visit the throne. I could not open the trailer door. I shoved and it moved only a few inches. Peeking out I saw the snow-filled awning sagging drastically and obstructing the passage. We had left the awning in place because the retractor was broken and to create more usable space outside the trailer. That our summer shade would become a trough for snow never occurred to us Californians.

Lloyd was able to push the door open enough for us to squeeze out sideways. We spent a half an hour bouncing the snow off the awning by poking it with our broom and a two-by-four. We had little success. For the rest of the winter I ran out at the first sign of a snowflake and started poking with the broom. Snow, I discovered, is mighty weighty.

Trying to keep snow, mud, and straw out of the trailer was a constant project. We removed our boots and encouraged visitors to do the same with little avail. The Silver Streak's dirt-colored carpet was a blessing.

The trailer was adequate, although days with cold wind and snow

Katherine Wells

made me antsy. We were warm enough wearing long johns, turtlenecks topped with T-shirts, sweatshirts, sweaters, fleece and flannel layers, though my feet were like ice at night. Lloyd bought me a pair of down booties to avoid contact with my "popsicle" toes. I enjoyed morning views of him returning from the throne shivering in bright red trap-door long johns. O pioneers!

Hiking in fresh snow was a source of great delight. Junipers and cholla huddled in thick white blankets, animal tracks skittered everywhere: bunnies, chipmunks, coyotes. Birds left fresh calligraphy. We made angel prints and had snowball skirmishes. Once friends came with cross-country skis and used our road as a course. And the snow nearly always melted off within a couple of days, so work continued steadily on the studio.

Because the studio is a Pueblo Style structure with no overhang, wisdom dictated the use of cement-based stucco plaster on the exterior walls. Wisdom lost. In the end we opted for mud plaster. Its simple beauty seduced us both. The visual and tactile appeal of mud walls shining with flecks of straw and sand and the softness of earth made people want to touch them.

We knew mud plaster meant having to replaster every year or two. We knew mud was a bad decision, but went our foolish way. By Christmas most of the exterior had a "scratch" (first) coat of plaster. The ingredients we used were dirt salvaged from leveling the site, sand, mule manure that served as a binder, which we obtained from a neighbor, water, and finely chopped straw.

For Christmas cards I cut miniature petroglyph shapes from sheet-metal scraps left over from construction and stuffed them into envelopes along with a little handful of straw. When they were opened, bits of straw flew out. I hoped my friends would enjoy the humor.

Just before Christmas my friends Jean and Joel and their teenaged son, Paul, came to visit. We had nearly a foot of snow when they arrived. The weather was inhumanly windy and cold. They planned to sleep in their old Chevy Suburban, but with no heat they would have frozen. We made up the banco for Paul, and Jean and Joel slept on the floor in down sleeping bags. Because the temperature was near zero, Ringo stayed inside and wandered from sleeper to sleeper. Wind nudged the trailer. We could see our breath. Only Paul slept well.

On Christmas Eve miles of luminarias with candles glowing in sand-filled paper bags lined the paved road. Driving the curves of asphalt through them with the car lights off was otherworldly. People from the community worked together that afternoon to set them out and light them at dusk. An old and beautiful tradition in this corner of the world.

New Mexicans go all out with Christmas decorations and strings of lights. Nearly every home had them. Even the shabbiest trailers were lit with hundreds of bright bulbs. Many homes had elaborate roof or yard ornaments. Frosty the Snowman shared the stage with wizened magi. Reindeer and camels jostled for space. Everyone vied for the Christ child's attention.

On Christmas Day the cold stung, but the sky was clear and the sun bright. Lloyd and I went to the Matachine Dance at San Juan Pueblo. I learned that this was their only non–Native American dance. The Matachine tradition originated among the Moors in North Africa who introduced the custom into Spain almost eight hundred years ago. From there the dance traveled to Mexico and later up the Rio Grande to what is now the state of New Mexico. Juan de Oñate's cohorts probably introduced the dance in the earliest years of colonization.

The dancing men wear black clothing topped by black headdresses that remind me of bishop hats decorated with long colorful ribbons. Masks obscure their faces. A small girl dressed in white representing La Malinche, an Indian woman who traveled with Cortés, dances with them.

The dance's repetitious fiddle music and beribboned costumes are a strange departure from traditional Pueblo dances such as the Turtle Dance that I witnessed at the pueblo the next day. The Turtle Dance is traditionally danced at San Juan Pueblo on December 26th. Scores of men danced and chanted wearing embroidered cotton kilts, sashes, moccasins, feathers, paint, amulets, sprigs of pine boughs from a sacred mountain nearby, and turtle shells tied to the outsides of their knees. I saw no evidence that the men felt the cold even though their torsos and arms were bare. Drummers provided a precise rhythm for the dancers. It was a mesmerizing sight under winter sun.

The Turtle Dance made me keenly aware of how little I knew about the pueblos. There is a lot that no outsider can ever know. The indigenous people's experience with the early Spanish taught them to keep their culture and religion sequestered. Some of their early encounters with anthropologists and explorers like Walter Fewkes left bitter feelings. Early investigators of Native American culture sometimes betrayed secrets and divulged esoteric knowledge.

I thought about the fact that I held a deed to land sacred to their ancestors, who had no concept of deeds or personal property but saw that land as part of their domain. Though I did not know all the circumstances, I knew my parcel had become part of the Sebastian Martin Spanish land grant around 1712. Sebastian Martin's heirs subsequently lost the land to unscrupulous Anglo lawyers in the late nineteenth and early twentieth centuries.

Why hadn't people from the pueblo worked together to buy my site or to persuade the government or a foundation to buy the parcel for them? Or banded together with other Tewa-speaking pueblos to purchase it? Did the petroglyphs on the mesa mean anything to present-day Tewa? Did they still identify with any specific images? Did they have any idea what a vast treasure of petroglyphs existed a short distance away? A parade of questions thrummed in my brain as I stood in the plaza at San Juan watching the Turtle Dance. The movement of the men's feet and the serene expressions on their faces were timeless. How many generations of men had performed this ceremony on this spot?

I was moved to see boys as young as three or four being initiated into this dance layered with meaning expressed in clothing, ornament, chant, and ritual dance. The tiny ones looked cold and a little confused but did their best to emulate the adults' movements. Now and then a father paused to straighten his small son's headdress or a mother would move in to tighten a sash with solemn but reassuring gestures.

How might I get to know someone in the pueblo who would have the answers to my questions? I understood that one did not barge in like you might in the Anglo world and say, "Hi. Let's talk about the petroglyphs." Any conversation had to be on pueblo terms and in pueblo time. Their worldview was radically different from mine. Questions could wait.

The week after Christmas we had air temperatures as high as sixty degrees. The snow melted and then it rained—an unheard of event in midwinter. Lloyd's truck could not negotiate the quagmire of our dirt road. My Vista was able to churn a path up to the driveway entrance, but the driveway itself was a sea of muck. We had to slog through the mud on foot to get to the trailer. The mess made doing anything difficult.

Except for a few day-trips, occasional movies, and dinners out, Lloyd and I had seldom been off the property since our arrival in June. We decided to go to Baja California where the weather would, we thought, be warm and dry. Lloyd had never explored much of Baja. I had never been to any of the spectacular cave painting sites there that every rock art buff longs to see. Lloyd agreed to go in search of cave painting sites near San Ignacio in the middle of the peninsula.

I put Ringo in a kennel near Española and we headed for Arizona. I had misgivings about leaving the dog there because she had never stayed in a kennel before, but there were no other good options. The place was clean and its owner seemed caring, but Ringo looked forlorn when I left her.

We went south through Arizona in beautiful weather and enjoyed a few days of respite. Unfortunately, new storms began to pound northern Baja and our return trip took a couple of days longer than anticipated because of washed-out roads and bridges and ferry delays. I called the kennel to check on Ringo as soon as we got to southern New Mexico. In disbelief I learned that she had died of something like a stroke. I was torn with grief and guilt. She had trusted me. I knew she felt abandoned when I walked away from the kennel. Yes, she was fourteen years old, a goodly age for a beagle, but she was in good health and I had no doubt that the stress of staying in the kennel had killed her.

We buried Ringo about one hundred yards from the trailer. I was inconsolable for weeks. Lloyd was annoyed when I didn't snap out of it, but the feeling that I killed her would not leave me. Later Lloyd finally began to understand my devastation. A couple of months later out of the blue he said, "She really did trust you, didn't she?"

The bright note from Mexico, at least for Lloyd, was a kitten. One day we pulled off the road in the desert far from any town to get sodas out of the back of the car. A tiny tabby ball of fluff yowling like a full-sized tiger accosted us almost immediately. The kitten appeared out of nowhere. Lloyd rummaged in the cooler for some goat cheese we had bought. The cat attacked the morsels with the desperation of the starving. When he could eat no more the feline yowled for attention. Lloyd obliged him.

There were no signs of human life in the desert around us. Lloyd wasn't about to leave the waif there, so we made a place for him in a box behind the front passenger seat. I like cats but try to keep my distance because I am allergic to them. Despite that, "el gato" crossed the border sleeping in my jacket pocket while Lloyd lied to the customs official.

Back home I named the kitten Qaddafi because he was a terrorist. He liked nothing better than leaping onto my leg with no provocation and planting four sets of well-honed claws into my flesh. Lloyd thought Qaddafi was an absolute darling. He grew to be tough and macho enough to give the coyotes pause.

The mud had dried up by the time we returned from Baja. Lloyd began working on the studio windows and thinking about the floor.

Five

I felt depressed after our return from Mexico for reasons other than Ringo's death. The thirty-foot Silver Streak seemed to shrink by the month. Things were mostly okay in the daytime. Lloyd and I were outside a lot. Evenings were thorny. There was no place for us to escape from one another. We had a small TV that Lloyd liked to watch for a couple of hours. His hearing was not very good, so the volume had to be high. As a young man in the Marines he had worked too close to helicopters without ear protection. Lloyd said he always had the sound of a million crickets in his head. He had tried hearing aids, but they irritated him and helped little. I seldom wanted to watch the TV programs Lloyd liked, and with the volume up, even the news drove me nuts.

By January I knew that I could not retain my sanity and stay in the trailer another winter. I sulked a lot and Lloyd snapped at me about small things—old food in the fridge, a pair of lost socks, where had I put his glasses. Finishing the studio and having the kind of house we wanted to build ready to occupy by the next winter seemed about as realistic as a trip to Jupiter.

Lloyd mentioned the possibility of moving into the studio when everything was finished. There was no way I would favor that. The space had no bath, no closets, cabinets, or kitchen. Living there would be chaotic and I didn't want to give up the hard-won territory where I looked forward to doing art again. What were the alternatives, I mused?

Around that time we were invited to dinner by a neighbor a mile or so down the road. Ellen had a small house where she spent her winters. The rest of the year she lived in New York. Her house was about eight hundred square feet with two small bedrooms, a bath, and an open living room, dining, and kitchen area. I would be fine if we had a space that size, I thought.

The idea struck me that Lloyd and I should consider building a small house that would be comfortable to live in until we were ready to consider the "dream house." Then the small house could become a rental. Lloyd and I discussed the idea. He was happy enough living in the trailer and willing to continue there indefinitely.

I suggested that we divide the property on the north side of our dirt road into two parcels, one for each of us. He could take the upper parcel, which had a superb house site, and I the smaller, lower piece, which had one small buildable area close to the road and another that would cost a lot to access and seemed important to leave untouched because of the petroglyphs nearby.

Lloyd was open to the idea, but did not want the job of getting a house up and ready to live in before the next winter. He had a lot of work left to finish on the studio and had retired to get away from construction under pressure. "It'll be your baby," he said. Gulp.

Could I make a house happen without Lloyd? Building in New Mexico, we had already learned, was a lot different than in California. People were less reliable about showing up and finding materials was aggravating because we lived off the beaten path. I knew nothing about construction except what I had learned from the studio. Still, I had owned a small business for almost ten years once and I was a good organizer. What could go wrong? Lloyd joked.

Somewhere we had learned about a contractor, Tom, who had experience with straw-bale building. What could I lose by talking to him? Lloyd agreed to be a part of the construction by doing what's called the "gray work," the part involving layout, footings, and slab, if the contractor agreed to the arrangement. I found the contractor's phone number and made an appointment to meet with him in Santa Fe.

Katherine Wells

We talked with Tom about the kind of house I had in mind. Then he took us to see a straw-bale project he had worked on. The structure was impressive. Tom believed in building with straw because of its environmental appeal and he was eager to get in on the ground floor of what he thought was going to become a popular construction trend. We discussed square footage, schedules, and straw sources, and we agreed to meet again when I had a set of plans.

My idea was a simple rectangular structure in northern New Mexico style with a pitched metal roof. The house would have two small bedrooms, one to be used as an office and guest quarters, a kitchen alcove off the living room, a fireplace, and built-in banco. I wanted to install radiant floor heating as we had in the studio because the system was efficient and quiet. Solar panels on the roof would provide most of the heat for the floor. Big windows in the front would allow for solar gain and enjoyment of the view. There would be a carport and a storage building for the water pressure tank, tools, and excess furniture that had been in a storage unit.

The plan was to begin in June so we could be living in the house before winter. Tom said that with a good crew the job could be done in three months. Plenty of time, I thought.

I began drawing and redrawing, changing dimensions, trying to design rooms that would be comfortable but not too large. I purchased books that gave me ideas and necessary information about kitchen, bath, and closet design and dimensions as well as other important elements. Lloyd went to Santa Fe with me to look at ready-made windows and doors. He critiqued the plans and helped me refine them. I found the process scary, but also exciting, even fun. If I couldn't be doing art, designing a house was a good diversion.

Lloyd continued work on the studio. After a long search, we found just the right door for the structure in an Albuquerque antique shop. It was an old, handmade Mexican door with remnants of blue paint, a tradition in New Mexico. Blue, people long believed, would keep witches and evil spirits away.

We crammed the door into the back of the Vista for the trip home. Lloyd's knees were under his chin as he drove. Having a door with a sense of age was important to him. One of the aesthetically appealing features of straw bale is that the medium has the soft, organic look of adobe. The studio would blend in with the terrain and the history of the area. For us creating the studio was an exercise in art as well as function. A building we could be proud of; one that honored the place.

Staring out the trailer window at the Key Rock one day I realized it had been a year since we first saw the property. My love affair with the land had not abated. I thought I had seen the vast majority of the petroglyphs by then, though I often had the surprise and delight of discovering some new treasure. One of the most elegant images I found in the early months was that of a mountain lion on a large, slightly concave, silvery-brown boulder in a commanding position overlooking the river. He measures nearly five feet from head to end of tail. All twenty toes are exquisitely etched.

Unlike every other Native American lion image I had ever seen in books, his head faces the viewer rather than being drawn in profile. Small, triangular "rays" encircle his head. A snake slithers across his neck. The petroglyph is mysterious and powerful, alive with meaning that eluded me. It was a mystery: did the big cat date back to the Pueblo IV period or was it from the early Historic era? Never did I wish so keenly for a direct line into the mind of a work's creator.

The mystery compounded when I found three small Historic-period glyphs of what are obviously heraldic lions rearing up on hind legs with tails curving over their backs, faces looking out at the viewer. They are crude and only lightly pecked, but there is no mistaking their European origin. Were they made by Spaniards roaming the hills or by Native Americans who had seen the image on a coat of arms and been intrigued by the design? More likely the latter, I thought.

Then, months later the mystery was compounded again. I happened on a much larger, finely engraved Spanish lion on a hill by itself in an area almost devoid of petroglyphs. He is roughly two feet long and has a distinct feeling of animation, in contrast to the more static mien of most prehistoric animal images. The feline faces north rather than east or south as most Pueblo IV period glyphs do. The lion seems more like art for the sake of art than image as invocation or shamanic magic.

Large Puebloan mountain lion
petroglyph with unique sun-like head.

Stylized heraldic Spanish lion image. An outstanding
example of Historic period petroglyphs.

Maybe the glyph was a territory marker or homage to the king of Spain. Patination places the beast in the early Historic period. Questions spun in my head. This cat was by far the most compelling Historic-period petroglyph image on the site and one of the best anywhere, I felt.

March came in like a lion and went out like a whole pride of the beasts. April followed with the same, nearly constant whine of wind. Though we had had windy days now and then, the intensity was all but unbearable in March and April. Gusts endlessly pounded the Streak from the southwest, setting my teeth on edge and making me antsy and irritable.

The wind made hiking unpleasant enough to keep me trailer bound. I fumed and tried to read novels, write letters to friends, work on planning for the upcoming house project, or otherwise occupy myself as wind assaulted the Streak. Lloyd and I took off for an afternoon movie in Santa Fe now and then. Sometimes I baked cookies thinking comfort food would take my mind off the wind. "It will be okay when I have a house; it will be okay when I have a house," I repeated, pacing the length of the trailer.

Lloyd tolerated the torment better than I. The studio windows and door were in so he could work on the interior plaster, build a sink cabinet, and finish other jobs. There was little I could do to help. I longed for the day I could get my art materials out of storage and move into the studio.

In late April I was able to venture out more. A variety of wildflowers adorned the mesa after heavy winter moisture. From then through June I was treated to a host of blossoms: vetch, Indian paintbrush, primrose, penstemon, globe mallow, yucca, cliff fendlerbush, prickly pear, claret cup and cholla cacti, and other flowers in yellows and purples, the names of which I could not find. Rice, buffalo, and gramma grasses greened up and gave the mesa a brighter hue.

A visitor even showed me cochineal growing on the pads of prickly pears. The insects looked like bits of white lint clinging to the base of the cactus pad spines. I carefully picked one off. Rubbing it between my fingers produced drops of crimson as though I had stuck my finger. I remembered that cochineal dye from Mexico became a major phenomenon in Europe in the sixteenth century. Never before had kings and queens enjoyed garments in such luscious shades of red.

Katherine Wells

Lloyd came in the trailer one day in April and told me I had a visitor. Perplexed, I went outside and was greeted by a small, black, cocker spaniel–like mop of a dog sitting nearby cautiously wagging his tail. Where had he come from? Lloyd didn't know. He just showed up. He was the first of many mutts who arrived at the door or at the bottom of our road over the years, often half-starved. I wasn't sure I wanted another dog, but this one would not take no for an answer.

Sadly, unwanted pets are frequently abandoned on the roads of New Mexico. Many New Mexicans, at least in rural areas, do not perceive of dogs and cats as pets. They are farm animals with jobs and those who do not perform get the boot. Once a neighbor offered me a very expensive young Alaskan husky he had bought as a watchdog. The pup was a big eater, but a slacker at his duties. Also, when we first arrived in New Mexico, many people had yet to develop the habit of spaying or neutering animals, which compounded the problem. For some the procedures were too expensive. Others seemed indifferent. Some men were opposed to neutering dogs and cats on the grounds that it would take away their "machoness." Even Lloyd was reluctant to deprive Qaddafi of his "jewels." Some of these animals find homes; many end up in overflowing shelters and are euthanized. Cars hit some. I managed to find homes for all but two who came to me in the first few years—one as big as a Great Dane with no socialization at all and one an old, very sick female. Those two went to the shelter and were, no doubt, put down.

Shaggy Dog, as I named the cocker spaniel–like dog, was the most irrepressibly cheerful creature I ever met. His curly black locks were always a snare for burrs, pieces of tumbleweed, and other plants. Sometimes he looked like a collection of walking vegetation, but he was never less than happy. He shadowed me on walks and soon moved into Ringo's house.

Another perennial problem we struggled with was trash. At that time there was no trash collection in the rural areas of the county and the nearest dump was thirty miles away. We composted and did other things to minimize our trash as much as we could, but refuse was an endless dilemma. There were no dumpsters around, and the concept of recycling was still an alien notion.

In addition to our own trash, litter at the bottom of our road was a perpetual aggravation. I often wrote nasty letters in my head to Anheuser-Busch while picking up cans and the shards of zillions of bottles because Budweiser was far and away the most popular brand of beer in New Mexico. Anheuser-Busch made boatloads of money on Bud every year in the state, but would not support a bottle deposit bill in the legislature. The litterers were culpable, but so too, I fumed, was the don't-give-a-damn corporate behemoth.

I sometimes thought local people just didn't care, didn't have any pride. Some, I am sure, did not care, but another element figured in. In the past, nearly all the trash was biodegradable. Anything edible was fed to pigs, chickens, or dogs. Everything else—clothes, shoes, saddles, tools—were used and reused down to the last nub. What remained was burnable or could be pitched to degrade into the earth.

Additionally, people did not consume as much "stuff" as we do now. Nobody had twenty T-shirts, a dozen pairs of pants, and ten pairs of shoes in the closet. Most folks didn't even have a closet. Maybe some of the local populace hadn't figured out yet that glass, aluminum, plastics, and most modern trash doesn't degrade.

People frequently left bags of trash, old tires, and even dead animals on our land. Neighborhood dogs invariably ripped open sacks with food smells and scattered debris everywhere. Picking up dirty diapers, Styrofoam meat trays, half-eaten tortillas, bloody tampons, condoms, cigarette butts, and evidence of drugs was a disgusting job.

And what to do with it? I am not proud to say that Lloyd and I sometimes took garbage to town and stuffed the bags into dumpsters belonging to local businesses. Many other people were apparently doing the same because there were regular articles in the local newspaper quoting merchants who complained. They began agitating for county pick up of trash, which began a couple of years later.

Lloyd and a helper finished the final coat of exterior plaster on the studio in May. The surface was gorgeous. Women, we learned, were traditionally

Katherine Wells

The completed studio building with mud-plastered walls.
Photo by the author.

the plasterers of adobe houses in Native American and Hispano cultures. They used their hands to spread and smooth the mixture of clay, sand, chopped straw, manure, and water. I liked that idea, but only as an idea. Besides, Lloyd was an artist with a trowel.

The finished walls were truly sensual. Everyone who visited automatically ran their hands over the surface as though touching velvet. Maybe a memory of the tactile pleasures of mud from childhood or a subliminal connection to the earth lost to most of us in our manufactured world made people reach out. No one who saw the building without knowing in advance ever guessed the walls to be straw bale rather than adobe.

Lloyd still had garage doors to build and interior plastering to finish in the garage/workshop half of the building. There were no garage doors on the market to complement the building, so he decided to design and build them himself. Lloyd never ceased to amaze me. Over the years I learned that there was nothing the guy couldn't make, and make beautifully, out of wood. The craftsmanship of everything he did was superb—including cooking!

I did a lot of the meal preparation during the building process, but Lloyd was by far the better cook and enjoyed the job much more than I. We were both happier when he was the chef and I the shopper, sous chef, and clean-up crew. Lloyd was a bred-in-the-bone foodie and an ectomorph who could eat outrageous amounts of food with impunity.

When we met, Lloyd and I had both lived alone for many years. My dinners were often takeout, leftovers, and canned soup. But even for himself, Lloyd prepared haute cuisine. He was never happier than when tucked into a rare steak dinner or an exquisite pasta dish he had fixed. Even though he ate hearty breakfasts the man was often hungry by midmorning. Many times he looked at me hopefully with his blue eyes atwinkle and said, "It's always lunchtime somewhere."

When I first knew him Lloyd's adoration of food astonished me. I was no slouch as a chowhound, but he had a very discerning palate and a willingness to lavish lots of time on food preparation and presentation. Sushi arranged on a plate with all the artistry of ikebana. Enchilada sauce made with fresh tomatillos, lamb chops poised on garlic mashed potatoes, grilled vegetable kabobs, colorful Greek salads. Eating what he cooked was often a satisfying visual as well as gustatory experience. I tended to save my middlebrow food feats for Christmas or Thanksgiving dinners, but Lloyd entered the kitchen as though it were a sacred space every day. Food as art. Food as religion.

That spring we met with Jay and Helen Crotty, directors of the Archaeological Society of New Mexico's Rock Art Field School, about recording the petroglyphs. They had recorded major sites in the state and their expertise was widely acknowledged. Helen was close to finishing her PhD dissertation at UCLA on New Mexico kiva murals, which are akin to petroglyphs. Jay's forte was surveying. Part of his job was to figure out how to divide up the 188 acres into logical chunks that could be recorded by the approximately thirty volunteers Jay and Helen would train and supervise the last two weeks of June. Not an

Katherine Wells

easy task given the radically up and down, arroyo riven, boulder clotted terrain.

In the end Jay cut the parcel into twenty-seven sections that would be assigned to teams of four people. Together Jay and Helen, who were volunteers themselves, did all the preliminary planning and organizing. The group would camp out at a group campground by a river about twenty miles away and carpool to the site, arriving no later than 7:00 a.m. each day. Everyone would work in the field until noon or so when the heat threatened to flatten the hardiest and the midday light made recording difficult. They would all return to the campground for lunch, a swim, and paperwork pertaining to what the teams recorded that day.

Each evening Jay and Helen planned a lecture or slide show about various aspects of rock art. I looked forward to participating, although I didn't know how I would manage to juggle my time and attention between recording and the house project. Maybe I was overdoing the mother hen role, but I felt I had to keep pretty close tabs on the house's progress. The charm of trailer life had long since worn off.

May's warm weather was like a shot of adrenalin for Lloyd. He planted a garden behind the trailer using straw bales to shield the plants from the wind. He put in tomatoes, peppers, squash, carrots, onions, lettuce, chard, corn, and sunflowers as a border. In front of the studio he planted flowers: petunias, cosmos, marigolds, and other annuals that assured bright hues. After a long, color-starved winter we were buoyed by the sight of green shoots popping up. Lloyd had a natural touch with plants and they flourished under his careful hands. By June we had lettuce and chard on the table. The anticipation of homegrown tomatoes in August was almost enough to send Lloyd into an old-fashioned swoon.

We found an injured, starving dog at the bottom of our road one day when we came back from a trip to town around the first of June. She wouldn't let us touch or even approach her. Her black tongue indicated that she was part Chow, a popular breed in New Mexico, but she looked more like a wild dingo. A generic New Mexico mutt, I decided.

We took food and water to the dog daily. After a while she let us pet her. She followed us up the road after a few days and met Shaggy

Dog. She was instantly in love. I had never seen a moony dog before, but she definitely mooned around Shaggy. They were a motley pair, but very compatible. Comparing them to a couple of little pugs wearing Pendleton wool coats I had seen in Santa Fe, I decided these two were my kind of dog. I had been petless most of my urban and suburban years but discovered that having dogs was a joy. They made great hiking companions, and I came to appreciate them as kindred souls in a way I never had before.

I named the girl Ginger because of her color and made an appointment to have her spayed. She had filled out with regular food and looked much better than when she first arrived, but I didn't want to keep her. One dog is plenty, I thought. The vet examined her injured right front leg and said the wound could not be fixed. She would limp and eventually arthritis would set in, but she was only about two years old. In spite of her limp she was a dedicated rabbit chaser and had a sweet personality. Ginger would make somebody a fine pet. I took her home and began trying to find a new owner for her, thinking maybe one of the thirty Rock Art Field School volunteers would want a dog.

We had more meetings with Tom as plans moved along to begin a small house in June. In March I had electricity routed from a nearby utility pole to the house site. I scheduled a well driller for early June. We expected the bulldozer work for the house to begin the first of June, but Hutchinson, the man contracted for the job, didn't show. He said he was hung up on another job and would arrive as soon as he could—probably a couple of days. A couple of days turned into a week, then ten days. I was chewing my nails. Tom and Lloyd seemed unconcerned. They had other jobs to do.

Hutch finally arrived and did an excellent job of installing the septic tank and preparing the leach field, leveling the site, digging the footings for the house, and putting two culverts in the driveway. Tom and Lloyd liked Hutch, but he drove me buggy because he was a real motormouth. I was never sure how much I paid for his yakking time.

When Hutch finished Lloyd began the rest of the prep work for the footings and the plumber came to begin the rough plumbing.

Katherine Wells

The well driller came a week late. I was beginning to think everyone in the state came a week late. Three people had recommended Larry to me as the best driller around. He set up his rig and went to work. On the first day problems arose. Big voids between boulders underground kept the drill from working. Larry brought endless sacks of a material called bentonite to fill them, but the stuff disappeared into the bowels of the earth. On the third day Larry packed up and departed, telling me to get somebody with different equipment. "But you can't leave," I screeched, jumping up and down in the road. Larry's truck disappeared around the curve in a trail of rising dust. I felt like the woman in Edvard Munch's famous *Scream* woodcut.

You cannot build a house without a water supply. We had to have water for the concrete pour, testing plumbing, plastering, and other purposes. Most of all I had to know that I would have a viable well to service the house. A house without water is not very useful and running a line from the well by the trailer would have required a lot of difficult, expensive, and scarring excavation.

When I calmed down I unwadded the piece of paper Larry had pressed into my imploring hand. It had the phone number of another driller Larry knew, Kevin, who was the only one within seventy-five miles who had the right equipment. Kevin couldn't come until mid-August at the earliest, more likely September. Groan. Time to come up with Plan B.

Lloyd suggested getting a few hundred feet of cheap water pipe and running a temporary line from the well we already had down to the house site. We would have to dig a shallow trench under the road, but that was not a big deal. The rest of the distance the pipe could be exposed since it was summer. I couldn't think of a more practical solution so we proceeded, but not having the real well in made me extremely nervous.

I had told Tom that I wanted to use local help as much as possible. There was no problem finding workers. We needed only one skilled carpenter in addition to Tom and two or three unskilled laborers since we were subcontracting the electrical and plumbing work. Chris, a young man from New Hampshire who lived a few miles away, got the carpenter job. In addition we hired Gerald, one of the López brothers who had worked on the studio, and a local Hispano named Pablo.

Pablo had pulled into our driveway in his dilapidated truck a few months earlier with one of his cousins. I could tell from their smell and behavior they had been drinking, and they wanted to sell us some miniature ladders they had made out of sticks. We didn't buy their creations, but told them we could use a real Pueblo-style ladder to climb up onto the studio roof if they could make one.

Pablo returned a couple of days later with an eight-foot ladder he had made. His workmanship was poor, but the object could be used. I bought it. Pablo was sober this time and told us that the man we bought the property from, an Anglo, was his uncle. Pablo, his mother and father, and a couple of siblings had lived in a trailer near where we sited the Streak for a few years when he was a kid.

His father was a war veteran and an alcoholic who had died when Pablo was small. From his body language I thought Pablo felt a lot of anger toward his dad. He now lived about five miles away with his mother, Esperanza. Extended family lived nearby.

Pablo was curious about the studio and asked if we had any work. I told him we would be starting a house in June. He did not have much in the way of skill, but Pablo was big and obviously strong. He said he was a good worker. I thought I should give him a try. We would have as much low-skill work to do on the house as we had on the studio. I asked Pablo to bring his mother by to visit someday. I very much wanted to meet her. They stopped by a few weeks later. Esperanza worked as a teacher's aide. She was quiet and said little about the time she had lived on the mesa. I hoped to get to know her better.

The Field School began on the third Saturday of June. Daily temperatures were in the mid-nineties by then. Hats were mandatory, sunscreen ubiquitous. I went to the group campground to join the others for training feeling like an eager first grader. People came from all over. Quite a few were from the East and West coasts. There was even a young woman from Canada. The group included teachers, college students, retired folks, photographers—an assortment. All paid their own way. Some had participated before and others were new.

I was impressed by the volunteers' interest, intelligence, eagerness, and the fact that they were giving their time and funds to have the experience of recording rock art. A couple of the volunteers gushed about how exhilarating it was to be recording a part of history. Others expressed quiet gratitude for the opportunity to see and record the petroglyphs. I began to feel like Queen of the Petroglyphs.

Much to my surprise Dr. J. J. Brody (Jerry) and his wife, Jean, came to work with us the first week. Jerry is a preeminent expert in Native American art of the Southwest. Jean has fewer diplomas, but her knowledge proved vast. She could hold her own with anybody. That they would donate their time to record rock art alongside the greenhorns amazed me.

Helen, Jay, and a couple of the old hands instructed us in what we needed to know. Though we would each have specific jobs, everyone needed to learn all the skills so we could fill in for others. The process involved photography, drawing, measuring, mapping, and recording various kinds of information on the data sheets. Accuracy was critical.

When the site recording was finished, all the information would be tallied and collated to give researchers the ability to see patterns in glyph location and the relative importance of one motif in the area compared to another, as well as this site compared to others. A person would be able to look at the data, go the site, and locate any given glyph with the mapping information we gathered.

Regrettably, we were working a few years before Geographic Positioning System (GPS) units were affordable. If we had had them the process would have been simpler and the location information we gathered even more precise.

The original copies and photos of our work would be given to ARMS—the Archaeological Records Management Section of the State Laboratory of Anthropology. As the landowner, I would receive duplicates of everything. The data we gathered would add appreciably to the historic record of local native people. If glyphs disappeared or were destroyed, at least there would be a record of what was lost. Protecting petroglyphs for future generations was the ultimate goal of our work.

The team artist was the key person for recording. In addition to making a clear drawing of each glyph, he or she had to record the information provided by others on the data sheet. Drawing was the most time-consuming job. Small details mattered because they were often not visible in the photos. For photography we used black-and-white thirty-five millimeter film that has a long archival life. The technology for digital photography was still in its infancy.

Other members of the team were responsible for taking measurements from glyphs to a chosen datum point using a one-hundred-meter tape measure. The tape was often draped over boulders and bushes, trailing up and down slopes. The measurers also assumed responsibility for mapping. Those who were mathematically inclined acquired mapping skills quickly. Others, like me, who didn't know an azimuth from an eggplant, took longer.

By Sunday afternoon everyone knew the basics and a little about Puebloan history. Jay and Helen had done the training enough times that they had the process down to a science. One of the places they had recorded was Chaco Canyon. Jay, I learned, was the codiscoverer of the Sun Dagger petroglyph at Chaco. It has become a world-famous solar marker. He wanted to climb Fajada Butte and Anna Sofaer volunteered to go along. She launched a career based on their find while he took none of the credit.

Jay assigned sections on Monday morning. My team leader, luckily, was Helen Crotty. Working with her was a huge treat because of her expertise. We began on Section One at the north end of the property where glyphs were sparse. Lloyd was working with the house project so I didn't have to think about it much for a few days.

Lloyd enjoyed meeting Jay and Helen, but I was disappointed that he had not developed much interest in rock art. We were surrounded by glyphs. Why didn't he find them more exciting? When I thought about how his face lit up around small airplanes or at a boat harbor, I understood. I stifled yawns in those places, but he was like a kid at the circus.

Section One, on a hill above a cluster of houses, was the only section near dwellings. Several dogs below barked themselves hoarse as we began to work. Part of our assigned area was an extremely steep hillside above a rutted dirt road. We had to call numbers and information back and forth to one another. One of my teammates, the photographer, did not hear well, but he had a very loud voice and talked endlessly as we struggled to stay upright and do our work on the slope.

About 10:00 a.m. a car slowed, then stopped on the road below us, a big, early 1970s era green Chrysler sedan. The driver, a Hispanic man

I judged to be in his twenties, eyed us for a few minutes and then got out of his car. He began yelling up at us. I could not understand all the words, but the gist of his rant was that we had no business being there, that we acted like we owned the world, that all we cared about was money, that this land belonged to his ancestors and we had stolen it from them, and who did we think we were?

The guy rambled on and on as I tried to figure out what to do. Helen and I exchanged looks. The photographer did not seem to understand what was going on and made a couple of inappropriate remarks. I wanted to tell him to shut the hell up. He was a sweet man, a good photographer, but socially dense.

I worked my way precariously down the slope, introduced myself as the landowner and told the young man my name and where I lived. He would not tell me his name and went on with his litany of grievances. I am not good at confrontation. My heart thumped madly in my chest as I struggled to keep from shaking. He needs to vent, I thought, so I kept quiet and let him talk. After a while he began to run out of steam. I think he realized that he sounded foolish.

I told Mr. X that we were recording rock art created not only by Indians, but everything done by humans. In that section there is a lot of Historic-era material. Fortunately, I had just drawn the images of some Spanish crosses that the young man could see on my clipboard. I told him about the project and that we were recording the history of his ancestors as well as those who came earlier, that we respected all the glyphs and hoped the community would support our efforts, and that all these people were volunteering their time.

He had calmed down by then. He still exuded hostility, but the situation was defused. I invited him to visit me. Mr. X just shrugged and took off. My take on the event was that he was probably undereducated, angry, unemployed, and believed that his culture was being destroyed by what he thought of as a bunch of rich Anglos moving into his territory. He might have thought we fit the profile. Later I mentioned the incident to a neighbor who knew him and learned that he was a guy with many problems. Mr. X must have needed a target that day and we looked like a bull's-eye. Replaying the scene in my head later I wanted to kick myself for not saying something to him in Spanish. Doing so might have made me seem less of an outsider to him. I was so undone by the confrontation that my brain shut down.

The following day we were working further along the hillside when three or four children who lived below climbed up to see what was going on. They ranged in age from six to eleven and were curious about my clipboard, drawings, and notes. We let them help with measurements and asked them to show us petroglyphs they knew about. We told them about the people who had lived there long ago and the importance of protecting the images. Later one of them picked up a sharp stone and began making her own glyph on a small boulder. The team cringed. Even though that is a major no-no we kept our mouths zipped. Building goodwill in the neighborhood trumped archaeological etiquette.

Once or twice during the Field School I went up to the group campground to help with the afternoon paperwork and enjoy the evening programs. Mostly, I let my teammates fill in for me so I could do whatever had to be done in preparation for the next day's work on the house.

Usually I needed to talk to Tom about the schedule for the plumber or the electrician, how the crew was doing, materials concerns—whatever came up. First there was a delay in getting some parts to finish up the installation of the radiant floor tubing for the heating system. One day became two, then four. Then one of the crew asked for time off because of a family illness.

Tom could tell I was already beginning to get hyper about keeping the job on schedule. "Let me share a piece of wisdom with you," he said with a chuckle. "Mañana doesn't mean tomorrow, it means not today." He had lived in New Mexico much of his life and was trying to drag me out of California time into New Mexico time, a zone all its own. I knew Tom was right and tried to lighten up. It worked until I thought about spending another winter in the trailer.

Shaggy Dog and Ginger followed me everywhere—to my team's section with the Field School, back and forth, up and down the road as I checked on the house project. Sometimes they wandered off to visit

Ginger, the best dog ever. Photo by the author.

other recording teams. I sang Ginger's praises to everyone hoping for an adoption. On the third day I tied a piece of florescent pink surveyor's tape around her neck bearing the message "please save me" written on it. Everyone said she was so sweet, but they couldn't take her home.

In my dogged determination to give the dog away, I stayed aloof, didn't pet her much, tried to avoid getting attached to her. She didn't buy it for a minute. One day as I scurried from trailer to house project to recording site Ginger began nipping me gently on the backside once in a while. I was so preoccupied I didn't pay much attention until the fourth or fifth nip. Huh, I thought. I stopped and wheeled around. Her expression said in plain English, "Hey, you're my person now, so how about a little affection?"

"You win," I answered. We had a little love fest sitting right there on the dirt road. That was the end of the nipping. I finally figured out that for outside dogs two would be much better than one for the sake of companionship. I never for a moment regretted keeping Ginger. Homely New Mexico mutt she was, but a world-class friend.

On the third day of recording, my team moved to Section Nine, one of the richest on the site. Like Section One, the terrain was steep and cactus infested. Everybody on the team had to help with measuring the distances from the chosen datum point to whatever rock we were recording. The process required a lot of clambering up and down hillsides and boulders, where we sometimes teetered like unschooled acrobats. I had an epiphany one day as I struggled to render a complex image while simultaneously straining to keep my balance with one foot on an unsteady, less-than-level rock and the other within an inch of dozens of cactus spines. I paused to wipe sweat from my eyes so I could see what I was doing and at the same time sparred with a crewmate about whether a little "thingy" on the right side of the rock he was measuring was natural or human made. "Natural," I said. "But it kinda looks like an atlatl," came the reply. The conversation continued as they often did when we tried to discern the intentions of a glyph maker or distinguish glyphs from the peculiar markings left on basalt rocks from their volcanic birth. My epiphany was that recording a glyph was sometimes as much work as creating one in the first place. Jay Crotty roved among the teams everyday to check that people were recording correctly on the data sheets, to help out wherever necessary and act as chief cheerleader.

The sun's ferocity at six thousand feet threatened to level us daily. I marveled that all the volunteers worked in such conditions just for fun. People mopped sweat, drank lots of water, and got on with the job. Teams competed for bragging rights about the best petroglyph find of the day or the worst horror story of meeting a rattlesnake or nasty encounters with cholla. Every recorder was having an adventure. I, too, would have volunteered to record other sites.

We had dinner at the home of a local volunteer the last night: enchiladas and beer, team jokes, promises to come again next year. Though no one could say for sure at that point, Jay and Helen thought we recorded

Katherine Wells

fewer than half of the glyphs on the site. After visiting our property the first time they had estimated the site would be a two-year project. There was no doubt now. In fact, to finish the job in another two-week session next year we would have to hustle. Jay had a major task ahead the next several months going over the data, tallying categories, and matching photos to data sheets. By rough count we had recorded nearly three thousand images.

Six

With my petroglyph-recording duties over, I could concentrate on building the house. In a few days Lloyd would be finished with what contractors call gray work, the concrete footings and slab. Then he would go back to making garage doors for what was to be his half of the studio building. He had another project in mind, too. Farther up the road on the acreage that became his in our property-division deal he was thinking of building a small structure. He wanted to try something round out of straw just to see how well the idea worked—maybe something along the lines of a Navajo hogan. Something cozy, he said.

By the Fourth of July I was ready to light a firecracker under Tom. His skills were good, but he was disorganized. He didn't plan ahead well. Sometimes he picked up lumber, bags of cement, or other materials in Santa Fe before coming to the job and arrived unconscionably late. The crew came at 8:00 a.m. If he didn't get there until 9:30 or 10:00 I had to be there to make sure the guys knew what they were supposed to do and had the materials they needed. If they didn't, I had to come up with a Plan B.

Over the weeks I became the de facto general contractor and made sure that materials were ordered ahead of time and that the job stayed on

The construction of the first house. Photo by the author.

track. There was no other way to move the project along efficiently. The crew was doing well even though a couple of them were green. Chris, the carpenter, was skilled and very knowledgeable. He became a crucial helper and a valued friend. Pablo turned out to be a willing worker, but he did not even own a tape measure or a decent hammer. I bought him a couple of things and Tom gave him an old tool belt. Sometimes keeping him focused was difficult because he was in love. One day after lunch, Juanita, the girlfriend, showed up on the job. One flash of her long black hair and Pablo was gone. He just dropped his tool belt where he stood and followed her like a love-struck pup. The other guys, of course, gave him no peace after that, though they had to tread lightly. He could have flattened any of them.

Another sticky issue with Tom was that of crew respect. He knew what he was doing, but he wasn't one of "the guys." At lunchtime they tended to eat by themselves and share camaraderie that excluded Tom.

Now and then I heard one of the crew make a derisive remark about him. They were working for me, not for him, and everyone worked hard. I had good rapport with the entire crew. In general I got along well with Tom, but I tried not to be too chummy in order to preserve an employer/ employee relationship. Every afternoon I brought a jug of iced tea and packages of cookies for them to enjoy on their break. I learned about their families and wives or girlfriends. I advanced money now and then if needed. I liked getting to know them and the feeling that they trusted me. They saw, as I helped sweep up and do other jobs during the day that I, too, knew how to work hard. I told them I didn't want to live in the trailer another winter if I didn't have to. Later I felt elitist for saying that. They lived in ratty trailers or dilapidated houses; they always had, and probably always would. I chewed daily on the blessings of my more privileged life and concluded that my economic advantage boiled down to two basic things: luck and education.

In short order the crew erected concrete block posts at the four corners of the house and one additional post in the center of the front and back walls. The posts were "tied" to the foundation with rebar and then filled with cement. Insulation material was placed around the outsides of the posts. We were ready to begin work on the bond beam around the top perimeter of the walls that would support the roof.

The building process was going smoothly enough even though I felt as though I had the proverbial tiger by the tail every day. When the bond beam was up Tom and Chris put wooden support posts in place. Window, ceiling, and interior framing followed. The cadence of hammers pounding and the whine of the table saw were odd symphonic counterpoints to the constant Mexican music playing on the battered, sawdust-covered radio.

A couple of vigorous summer rains pummeled us before work began on the roof. We had to protect the straw bales carefully until we were ready to use them. They were covered with bright blue plastic tarps and stacked in giant blocks in what was to be the driveway for the house. I checked for places rain might penetrate the plastic every time a cloud appeared. We ordered roof trusses to be delivered from

Albuquerque and metal roofing material from Santa Fe. I was anxious to have the roof on so we would be "dried in," a major milestone in any building project.

Putting up the trusses and sheathing them with plywood went smoothly, but installing the metal roofing was scary. The guys built special blocks to stand or kneel on as they worked to keep from sliding. The task would have been difficult, exhausting work under the best of conditions, but the heat made the procedure a nightmare in the August heat. I craned my neck, watching like a nervous mother, as they laid the metal sheets in place and screwed them down. I admonished the crew that if anyone did not feel safe he should come back to the ground. The guys all took their turns though. They developed the kind of esprit de corps that men do in battle.

Pablo's brother Luis came one day and asked if we could put him to work. He had experience at carpentry and electrical work, so I hired him.

A few weeks later another of the brothers, José, who lived next door to his mother and Pablo, disappeared. Pablo and Luis took a day off to look for him. Other members of the family joined the search. While they were gone, José's mentally disturbed and retarded teenaged son vanished. The boy lived with Pablo and his mother, Esperanza. Pablo and Luis came to visit me early that evening to warn me about him. I was cleaning up at the house while Lloyd was at the trailer taking a shower before dinner. They were afraid that José Jr. had killed his father because he hated him and was mentally unstable. I had seen Junior one time. The look on his face chilled me. It was both dark and wild.

Pablo and Luis said the boy knew the mesa well and that he could be hiding somewhere among the hills and boulders. They were worried he might come to our trailer in desperation. The brothers didn't know if Junior had a weapon. I was shocked and a little frightened. Lordy, what am I doing here? I thought to myself. This was the stuff of bad dreams and B movies. Yet here it was on my doorstep.

The two men tried to maintain their stoic composure but both looked confused and scared. I hugged them and they hugged back. The gesture was simultaneously strange and comforting. Hugs would not

Katherine Wells

have happened under any but the most dire of circumstances because both were reserved and I was their employer.

The police found José's mutilated body the next morning and later that day they apprehended the boy. There was little doubt that Junior had killed his father. The son was taken to a mental institution rather than to jail. Lloyd and I went to the funeral at the Catholic church everyone in the area attended. Pablo, wearing a bandana covering his head as he always did, was one of the pallbearers along with Luis, wearing a suit, and other family members. Luis was poker-faced but Pablo looked stricken, as though he had been stabbed himself. I couldn't fathom how anyone in the family remained sane, especially Esperanza.

As a mother I could not imagine surviving such horror. The event was so far beyond my experience that I could not process it. How, I wondered, could a family go on? How many days, weeks, years before any of them could wake up in the morning without an image of father, son, blood to start the day? How long before they could go about their lives without being haunted by the hideous mix of love, murder, and unspeakable loss?

There was one positive note. When José died Pablo quit drinking forever.

After José's death I became more and more aware that tragedy was no stranger to local families. Weekly the Española newspaper featured horrific stories. A young woman raped and bludgeoned to death, then burned by three young men behind a local supermarket. An eighteen-year-old girl shot by her jealous boyfriend. A nine-year-old girl killed by a drug addict who broke in to her family's home. A small child injured when her parents' drug deal went wrong.

The stories were endless and appalling. Nearly all involved drugs or alcohol or both. My mind whipsawed between empathy and outrage that such crimes were tolerated without the community rising up to prevent such heinous behavior. Such crimes occurred in southern California, but I was little touched by them in my white, suburban neighborhood. In both areas I knew that law enforcement and education needed vast improvement.

September came, but the well driller did not. The straw bales were in place and the chicken wire sewn to them. Tom built the fireplace and was working on cabinets while Chris and Luis trimmed windows and the rest of the crew worked on other projects. We were ready for stucco outside and plaster inside. Still we had no well. Lloyd tried calming me, but my anxiety level was in the stratosphere.

By this time I could have written a tome about the exasperations of house building in general and in New Mexico in particular. People do not come when they say they will and do not call to tell you they will not or cannot come, or why. Or if they tell you why you get the same stories: the truck broke down; I had to go to a funeral; or, my favorite, I had to go to court. Materials do not arrive when vendors say they will. It's in El Paso. Be here in two days. Or, didn't the manager call you? Or, the manufacturer says they're back-ordered. Probably six or eight weeks. Were I given to hair pulling I'd have been bald by the time the walls were up.

After the umpteenth phone call I finally got a quasi-commitment from the well driller for the middle of September. When he finally showed up he completed the job in a couple of days. He only had to drill about 150 feet down and the quality of the water was excellent. Maybe I would not have to spend another winter in the trailer after all.

By the time the well driller finished his job the plastering crew had arrived. I chose white gypsum plaster with a soft, eggshell sheen for inside the house. The outside would be finished in an earth-colored stucco. The contractor and his crew applied the scratch coat on the outside first using a sort of gun attached to a hose and a machine that kept the material coming. They literally shot the stucco on. Two guys followed with trowels to smooth the surface. The process was fast and worked well because pressure from the gun forced the material into all the nooks and crannies in the straw.

The weather finally began to cool toward the end of September. Lloyd's carefully tended tomato plants in the garden cranked out red, juicy globes by the kilo. The days softened. Our perceptions grew sharper as

Katherine Wells

the sun slid south. Time tasted sweet like the tomatoes. I wanted to hold moments on my tongue and suck out the fleeting flavor.

We were at that stage of construction where the process seems almost finished except for the details. There the devil definitely dwells. During the early stages of building big jobs like putting up walls and roofs give the illusion that everything will be done quickly. The illusion blows up just when you think the end is in sight. Cabinets, finish carpentry, finish plumbing and electrical work, and many other end-stage tasks snail along. And you're beset with the inevitable glitches—tile badly installed, plumbing fixtures that don't arrive, wiring puzzles and the electrician gone AWOL. "Take a deep breath," I repeated to myself over and over like a mantra. I would prefer having a root canal every day to the anxiety of house building: driving thirty miles round trip to the hardware store for the third time in the same day; smiling after an innocent but very expensive screw-up by a crew member; wanting to slash your wrists after your own stupid $700 screw-up; sweating the threat of rain at the very worst time; chewing your nails to the bone because of endless unanticipated costs; worrying about injuries from carelessness; trying to smile in front of the crew when you want to whine or yell or tell them to go home and never come back.

Midpoint in the process I was sorry I ever started anything. Some days I wished I had settled for a mobile home. Who cares if it's made of plastic punched out by a cookie cutter and the walls outgas formaldehyde. So what if you live in something that has all the individuality of a Big Mac. I was ready to sign up for instant gratification. Moving into the house still seemed like a distant dream, a chimera I was destined not to reach by the first part of October. But by the middle of September all the maddening details suddenly began to come together. Insulation material still had to be blown into the attic, solar panels installed on the roof . . . but the list dwindled. My sense of being trapped in an unending nightmare dissipated.

That summer Lloyd had spent a few weeks finishing and installing the garage doors on the studio building and fussing over details like a tile countertop and sink installation. Then he took off a few days to go fishing up in Colorado. Stream fishing for brook trout was one of his passions in life and he needed a break from building. Maybe he needed a break from my daily litany of concerns and gripes about the house.

After his restful sojourn Lloyd began work on his idea for a round straw-bale structure up the road on his property. He studied the terrain in his deliberate way, then chose a site for the building among boulders and junipers with the best possible view of the mountains. With his careful plan in hand he set to work by himself.

Lloyd used native rock for the building's foundation. When he was ready to construct the rounded walls he gave each straw bale a slight curve by holding it and bending it with his knee. For the roof he constructed a shallow cone out of rebar that he winched into place with his truck and a little help from me. He insulated and then covered the cone with corrugated sheet metal that he aged with acid to an appealing rusty color.

Inside the structure Lloyd made a polished mud floor as people had in the region long ago. He mud plastered the walls inside and out. Because he designed the roof with a wide overhang Lloyd thought the outside walls could withstand the weather for several years.

The "hogan," as Lloyd dubbed the structure, was only sixteen feet in diameter. When finished the place looked as though it had been there a long time. The building reflected Lloyd's personality and philosophy: warm and calm and quirky but a little rough around the edges; a feeling for the past; age as an honorable state; good craftsmanship, but not fancy.

Though the hogan had no water source or electricity, Lloyd thought it would serve as guest quarters for the hardy. I thought the space would be his retreat, a.k.a. doghouse. Someplace he could go when he didn't want to deal with me or was feeling antisocial. In the end the hogan was a refuge, a place for solitude that was purely and uniquely him.

By late October the house began to feel like a house, and I began to get revved up about moving in. Though only about 1,200 square feet, my new domicile was palatial compared to a thirty-foot trailer.

Lloyd pitched in for the last few days to help seal the Saltillo tile on the floors, install towel racks, put sealer on the cabinets, and other last minute details. In early November we drove a rented truck up to the

Katherine Wells

Lloyd's "hogan" in winter. Photo by the author.

house filled with furniture and possessions that had been in storage. At last I had a real house.

Having a washer and dryer after eighteen months of lugging dirty duds to Española felt like the ultimate luxury, although the laundromat experience had its rewards. I liked talking to the local women about their kids who raced laundry carts while the mothers watched dryers spin as though watching numbing TV reruns. I watched Sikhs visiting the local Sikh community fold their gauzy turbans that were bigger than a queen-sized bedsheet. I wondered how they managed to wind yards of fabric neatly around their heads each morning before going to group meditation at 4:00 a.m. What if the folds got crossed or came out badly wrinkled? Did a Sikh ever have a bad turban day?

Having a toilet with no peat moss motes floating around and no drawer full of vaguely composted poop was the next best thing to living at the Ritz. The fixture I bought was of the water-saving 1.6 gallon per flush variety, which subdued my guilt about abandoning the composting toilet idea.

One of my first get-settled jobs was to make draperies and cushion covers for the built-in banco. I hauled my sewing machine out and set it up on the dining table. In three days I stitched simple monk's cloth drapes with loops at the top that hung from wooden dowels.

Lloyd needed curtains for the large windows of the hogan. He wanted a homespun effect and chose flax-colored burlap backed with white cotton. I offered to make the curtains for him but he said he would handle the job himself. I had to fight to keep my mouth and eyebrows under control when he told me. The guy could build a house, whip up a gourmet meal, or design an airplane, but his sewing experience was limited to sewing a button on a shirt. Lloyd's plan was to "glue" the curtains with fabric glue.

"Glue?" I asked.

I watched out of the corner of my eye as I went about my tasks and Lloyd spread the fabric out on the floor, wrestled the two layers into quasi-cooperation, and then applied spray-on glue. He took frequent breaks to ponder the resulting problems of unsightly wrinkles, lumps, and hems that did not stick.

Lloyd said he did not want me to do the job because I had so many other things to deal with. I thought maybe pride played a part in his decision. He wanted everything in the hogan to be made by him. After several tries he caved in. I warmed up my old Bernina again.

Neither of us had brought a couch to New Mexico, but with the built-in banco, a table, and a tribal rug on the tile floor in the living room, the house began to look warm and inviting.

We planned to go couch shopping in Albuquerque or Santa Fe but a jolting glitch arose when Lloyd received an unsettling phone call. He owned a small rental house on a one-acre lot in California that was suddenly vacated in disastrous condition. He decided he should go out and fix the place up to sell. Pronto. Getting the house and property into marketable condition would be a major job.

He thought he might be gone for two or three months.

A couple of days after the phone call, Lloyd left. I was taken aback by the sudden departure and felt a pang of sorrow as I watched his truck

Katherine Wells

disappear down the road. Lloyd was not a good communicator and I had been so consumed in house building that it would have taken a two-by-four to get my attention.

We had talked as he packed his truck. He said he had been missing the ocean; needed to spend a little time with the waves lapping at his feet. Maybe do a little fishing. Something like my need to see mountains and petroglyphs. "Okay, Kiddo?" he asked, grinning, putting on his favorite battered black cowboy hat. Lloyd looked so rakish I had to smile back. But there were tears behind the smile.

I felt that this was the end of the beginning of our relationship. I thought we would stay together, but knew it was time to put away the illusory hope of solid emotional intimacy that had seemed possible when we first met. In the upheaval of moving, the challenges of learning to live in a new terrain and culture, the struggles and excitement of building the studio and house, parts of our "ship" had foundered. Our eighteen months in the trailer had clearly taken a toll. We were suffering from togetherness fatigue. Lloyd and I had had a couple of wrenching rows during the summer, so we could both use some breathing space. He didn't say so, but I suspected he was bruised that we were moving into "my" house rather than "our" house. He liked being in control of things and I tried to be careful not to tread on his sense of autonomy.

I had learned the hard way, though, that always shoving my own needs into the background as many women of my generation still do, as I had long done, was not the answer. Lloyd's absence would give me time to settle in and enjoy the house alone for a while and to start working in the studio. It would give me time to think about Lloyd and me as a couple and where we were going separately and together.

By the time the house was finished I had met several women in the area including one or two I thought could become good friends. One was Joan, who had only recently moved to New Mexico. For years she was a designer and then she went back to school to become a psychotherapist. I liked her intelligence and ability to be outrageous in ways that made me laugh. I could talk to her about Lloyd and share experiences and insights about life as a newcomer in northern New Mexico.

Joan and I had dinner together now and then and I asked her to go couch shopping with me. We found a leather sofa with the texture of an

The first house completed. Photo by the author.

old bomber jacket. I hesitated to go ahead without Lloyd's opinion but in addition to being comfy I knew the piece would look good in the house. He later gave it his approval for looks and as a nap couch.

Sometimes I just sat on the couch for long periods and basked in the serenity of the house, the view, and the companionable silence. I felt great satisfaction with the way the house turned out: comfortable, but not small in feeling; simple, but aesthetically warm. As a space the structure was everything I hoped for. The days were a healing respite after the pummeling months of construction. That process was an over-the-top reminder of my lack of talent for handling big-league stress.

There have been few periods of such delicious calm in my life. I looked forward to Lloyd's return, yet at the same time wished the exquisite tranquility would last forever. The time gave me a chance to reflect and count my blessings, to consider how privileged I am to have been dropped on the planet when and where I was and to have the experiences and opportunities I had been given, and to enjoy the illusion that there would be a smooth ever after.

As winter approached most days were sunny and perfect for hiking. The dogs and I luxuriated in the keen air at an unpressured pace. I revisited places on the land that felt special to me in ways I could hardly name. One was a small arroyo near the trailer carpeted with sugar fine sand, sheltered by junipers. A small boulder there hosted two foot-long serpents undulating in unison toward eternity. Their dark coffee color suggested great age. Another secluded arroyo sheltered a petroglyph disk smoothed almost to oblivion by a millennia of intermittent water. A third locale featured a powerful image of a human female giving birth. Nearby, an equally powerful figure of a woman inside the outline of a bear paw stood watch.

Petroglyph of a probable birthing scene with baby emerging, tiny figures and germinating seeds.

Anatomically correct female image surrounded by a bear paw.

All of these glyphs and their surroundings resonated a sense of presence that I wanted to soak up, dissolve into. Historian Richard White says that landscapes do not speak to strangers. I would never know the flora and fauna, the stones, moods of sky and earth as the early people had, but I knew it better than I had known any other terrain. The urban landscape of Kansas City where I grew up and the plains of eastern Kansas where my parents were born, places I often went to stay with grandparents, aunts, uncles, and cousins during my childhood, had no enduring hold on me. Nor did the California of my adulthood. I felt like a part of this corner of New Mexico and would keep listening, hoping in time to decipher a few words of its language.

Katherine Wells

Picking up slick, river-rounded stones high above the Rio Grande, I tried to imagine the time eons before when there was water where I now walked. Sometimes I put a small white stone into my mouth to taste the smoothness, the centuries of water that had tumbled and worn it down.

Other days the dogs and I walked trails deep in fallen cottonwood leaves to reach the river where the dogs waded and scared up wild ducks. I cheered chevrons of geese heading south along the river's course, held my breath as an eagle perched in the top of a cottonwood watched me, felt the season shift and the sun loosen its fiery grip.

The Rio Grande is hardly a river at all by the standards of the Missouri or Mississippi. Some would scoff at its "Grande" status, but in this high desert the river is The Source, the reason that animals and humans from the ancient ones to me could survive the sere terrain. My neighbors watered their chile, corn, and alfalfa crops from acequias that were already in use when Europeans arrived. Mountain lions, badgers, and a host of other creatures still drank from the river at dusk or dawn. Those of us who live along its course sink wells that get water from the Rio Grande. Rio Madre. Rio Vida.

I reflected on what I had read about the Pueblo people's belief that all things must be kept in balance; misfortune comes when human affairs knock things out of equilibrium. Since the first human invented agriculture by intentionally planting seeds about ten thousand years ago things have slowly drifted more and more out of balance; now the planet's inability to cope with the imbalance we have created threatens us all.

Those who made the petroglyphs I so admire understood what my culture seems unable to grasp: that we are part of a Great System. I don't think I am romanticizing to say that the petroglyph makers and many of their descendents have a better sense of what's what than all the folks in gas guzzlers on the freeways. For all our technological prowess, people as a whole lack the will, the foresight, the wisdom to address the slow motion environmental catastrophe of our own making that is under way.

Handsome Dan's Boots, mixed-media sculpture. Photo by Pat Pollard.

A couple of weeks after Lloyd left, I entered the studio to work feeling eager and hesitant at the same time. Other than the house, a few Christmas ornaments were the only things I had created since three or four months before leaving California. My rational mind knew better, but a nasty little fear lurked that the muse was gone. Poof! Into the ether. I had had the feeling before. "Thee of little faith," I admonished.

Katherine Wells

The first day I sat quietly with some of the pieces I had brought from California. Would I continue to work in the same vein? Was something new brewing? How was my psyche processing this new place? In the past my work had reflected inner landscapes and my angst about the world we have made. Heavy stuff, most of it, but now and then leavened by humor.

Before packing up the studio in California I had begun a series of pieces that were just for fun. They were pairs of feet cast in a kind of plaster called Hydrocal—mine, Lloyd's, those of friends. I had attached them to the cutoff tops of real boots in a way that you could not tell where the boot stopped and the foot started. They were boots with ten toes to the pair that I decorated in various ways. Like Magritte paintings in 3-D. Cowboy boots, combat boots, knee-high zippered boots, kids' boots— all with toes. I would start with more of those I decided, just to flex my creative muscles. What came next would take care of itself.

Seven

The sounds were familiar. The high whine and twang of hundreds of halyards and nylon lines vibrating against aluminum booms and masts that stood like a small forest above us. A steady twelve-knot wind surging toward shore. Our footfalls made hollow reports on gray wooden boards as Lloyd and I walked past millions of dollars worth of luxury craft: chunky power cruisers known as "stink pots" to the sailing crowd, sleek sloops, cutters and ketches whose tall spars swayed in the wind. Whitecaps embellished the harbor under California's dazzling winter sun. Marina del Rey was one of the last places I would have expected to be in February of 1996. Lloyd and I passed boat after boat with cutesie names: Fred's Folly, My Fair Lady, Chapter XI, One for the Money. Lloyd's trimaran bumped at the rubber fenders attached to the last slip in the row, a poor relation to the fancy neighboring yachts.

I thought I was through with boats. My ex-husband Geza and I had shared a sailboat with friends in 1972, then purchased our own boat nearly a year later. Wanting a strong vessel we had chosen a thirty-six-foot steel cutter built in Australia. We planned to rebuild her interior and do some long-distance cruising. Eventually we did sail among the Channel Islands and to the tip of Baja California and up to the city of

La Paz with friends, but in the end the stress of the overhaul brought out the weaknesses in our marriage and was part of its downfall. When Geza and I separated he kept the boat.

Years later here I was again. Another man, another boat. Same ocean. At least I didn't own half of this vessel.

Even though New Mexico had been our home for more than three years Lloyd still subscribed to boating magazines. He had once owned a daysailer but harbored dreams of owning a "real" boat. I thought when we moved to New Mexico he had relinquished the idea. Instead, he towed the desire along when we came to the Land of Enchantment. Being nine hundred miles from the beach did not diminish his dream.

The previous November Lloyd had come to Southern California to visit two of his children. He mentioned before he left that he might look at a couple of boats. Given the impracticality of taking care of a boat at such a distance I thought that's what he meant. Look. Lloyd returned and announced that he had purchased the type of thirty-foot trimaran he had lusted after for decades.

My God, what possessed him? I asked myself. How the hell is he going to deal with a boat from New Mexico? Why didn't I see this coming? I felt hurt that he hadn't shared his intent with me. At times he was impulsive, but this purchase seemed premeditated.

The vessel was a homemade creation and lacked the sleek touches of a commercially made boat. Funky, I thought at first sight. Lloyd assured me she was solid and fast. When I climbed through the hatch and down into the salon my heart sank. The interior space reminded me of Lloyd's truck: masculine, more or less functional, with scant attention to amenities. A minimal and grungy galley, a head with only a curtain for privacy, small, scratched up portholes that admitted little light. A guy's boat.

Lloyd beamed with proprietary pride. I smiled and kept quiet.

"Wait till I get her spruced up," he said.

My relationship with Lloyd had changed substantially since our first year in New Mexico. We still enjoyed each other's company, but the level of intimacy and accord I had hoped for in our early days together had not developed. Lloyd had a well-defended inner fortress that was impossible

Katherine Wells

to breach. My own experience had been that opening doors and confronting my boogeymen were less painful and energy consuming than keeping them locked up. We were not like young couples figuring out who we were in the world, developing careers, and having children. We each had a sense of the importance of doing the things we wanted while the doing was good. He wanted to own a boat, goddammit, so he bought one. I wanted to create art and research petroglyphs and that's what I was doing. In a way we were like two kids at parallel play. Together but separate. We both got enough out of our relationship to make staying together worthwhile. I preferred what we had to being alone or looking for someone else. I had reached the point where the thought of starting over held little appeal. I had compromised, but did so consciously. And I had learned something with Lloyd: to set boundaries.

In my previous relationships with men I had allowed myself to be stepped on out of fear that I would be alone—as though that were the worst of all possible fates. A therapist I had worked with quoted a psychological edict that resonated for me profoundly. "The parent of the opposite sex," she said, "tells you who you are. The parent of the same sex tells you how to be that." My father's unspoken message was that I had little value. My mother, though she loved me unconditionally and was the kindest person I have ever known, was a poor role model. Like most women of her generation she tolerated whatever came with little resistance: alcoholism, philandering, squandering of income, and psychological abuse. Though my experience paled next to hers, I had tolerated unacceptable behavior from men in silence. That was over. I had learned where to hold the line.

I spent a few days on the boat with Lloyd helping him prepare to sail down to San Diego and later to Baja California. A couple of friends, including one with a lot of sailing experience, planned to go along. I was relieved because Lloyd had little deep water sailing experience.

The "captain" was in a state of high excitement when I left to return to New Mexico. "Be careful," I said, giving him a last squeeze when he dropped me at the airport in our rental car. His blue eyes shone like a five-year-old's at Christmas.

Lloyd sailed his boat, "Guadalupe," to Cabo San Lucas in Baja California in March of 1996. He had renamed the craft because of my interest in Our Lady of Guadalupe and had "Guadalupe" and "Española" painted on the transom. Only the geographically well-informed got the joke: Española is a long way from the ocean.

During Lloyd's sojourns I was able to concentrate on art. When I was alone and focused, time did not exist. The door of the studio was a portal to a niche in my brain where I suspended ordinary reality. For a while I basked in creative bliss.

My first real creative burst in New Mexico was born of sorrow. The horror of slaughter in Bosnia. The blood rivers of Rwanda. Closer to home in Española there were endless stories in the newspaper about young men killing other young people in senseless displays of barbarity. The violence eroded my sanity. I began casting around for a way to help me bear the pain of my species' penchant for killing: our collective death wish.

When we moved to New Mexico I became interested in the figure of Our Lady of Guadalupe as a cultural icon. She was omnipresent and seemed more popular and powerful than Jesus. I had been aware of her in California and on visits to Mexico, but I had never investigated her history. One thing that appealed to me was Our Lady of Guadalupe's appearance in the New World in the guise of an indigenous woman rather than a European. And the belief that she appeared to a poor Indian and spoke in his native tongue. I liked the idea that the bishop in Mexico City did what she told him to do—he built a church in her honor on the place of her apparition, a hill that had been a shrine to the Aztec goddess Tonántzin. Tonántzin is another version of the goddess Coatlicúe, "She of the Serpent Skirts," to me the most powerful goddess image ever created by humankind. With her necklace of skulls and snakes emerging from her headless neck, she evokes fear and awe.

The veracity of the Guadalupe story held little interest for me. Her history and symbolism, I thought, were perfect. As someone who grew up in and abandoned Protestant Christian tradition I had long thought it absurd that the feminine half of the human equation was almost absent from the faith. The church dragged Mary out of the closet at Christmastime for a few minutes, but left her to molder the rest of the year. Guadalupe represented the full power of the feminine shoulder

Katherine Wells

Large Guadalupe Image #2, detail of life-sized mixed-media sculpture with bullets used as rays, 57" x 20" x 7". Photo by Pat Pollard.

to shoulder with the masculine element. Her predecessors' credentials harkened back to humankind's earliest consciousness.

I wanted to use the image of Guadalupe in my work to express the despair I felt about the human race. Mary/Guadalupe was a mother. I am a mother. Mothers, I feel, need to stand up and resist the unspeakable violence in our culture. However, I thought I should not use Guadalupe, or Guad, as I came to call her, because I am not a Catholic, or even a Christian, for that matter. And I am an Anglo. I stewed about the dilemma for several weeks. At last I decided that if I used Guadalupe's image with respect and in a nontraditional way she could be a voice for my distress. She belonged not just to the Catholics, I felt, but symbolically to us all. She had, after all, shown up in Mexico before Martin Luther's famous cleaving of the Christian Church in Europe, which was the beginning of Protestantism.

My first piece was a life-sized image in which I used a mask of my face manipulated to reflect millennia of sorrow by emphasizing hollow cheeks and downcast eyes. I used my own face because it is thin and thin faces work better for expressive masks. Also I thought doing so lent another layer of meaning to the work. For the mandorla surrounding Guadalupe I attached gleaming four-inch-long rifle bullets without gunpowder that shone in horrific beauty. I created her clothing from painted cloth stiffened with plaster. Later I made three more figures on the same scale as companion pieces. I suspected that no one would buy them, but that was not the point. I had found a vessel to express my grief.

In late 1993 I attended a meeting a few miles down the paved road, SR 582, in a neighboring small village. A dynamic woman I had met named Rose invited me. Rose had wild red hair, keen intelligence, and a passion for her community. The gathering was about a gravel mine that had been opened in the traditional farming area by George Baker. He had already blighted an apple-growing community a few miles to the north with another gravel operation that left the terrain forever scarred. Baker went from area to area mining as he pleased, never reclaiming anything, never considering the impact on local communities.

Now he was mining gravel at the foot of the mesa where Rose's community had been since the 1700s. Baker had purchased 360 acres adjacent to the fields and homes of the neighborhood from a man who lived nearby. The villagers were understandably riled.

Every day great clouds of dust rose from the mine and drifted onto fields and homes. When the wind blew the community suffered dust storms that could be seen for miles. A couple of asthmatic children in the community experienced an increase in breathing problems. Farmers complained that the dust covering the leaves of crops inhibited growth.

Bulldozers and backhoes droned all day. The incessant "beep beep beep" as they backed up from dawn till dusk got on everyone's nerves. Eighteen-wheel trucks sped up and down the narrow two-lane road through the village endangering kids on bikes, pedestrians, dogs, stray livestock, and other vehicles. Many residents had broken windshields from flying gravel. The community decided to fight back.

Neither the county or the state regulated gravel mining then. The New Mexico Department of Transportation (formerly the New Mexico State Highway Transportation Department), or NMDOT, did not enforce speed, truckload limits, or tarping regulations on SR 582. Baker was a good friend of Pete Rahn, the secretary of NMDOT. Most of what Baker mined was sold to NMDOT for road building. Owing to his wealth and power, what Baker wanted, Baker got.

Over time I began to learn more about the man. Baker's father had come to Española as a poor young man and had become wealthy. George inherited the mantle. In spite of his money Baker lives in a middle-class house and does not flaunt his wealth. He loves power and manipulation. Rose thought he was about sixty-five years old.

Many of the Hispanos in the area were reluctant to raise their voices against Baker because he employed hundreds of people. Any time anyone said a word against Baker's mining activities he howled that jobs would be lost if any restrictions were imposed upon him. No one in our group wanted to deprive anybody of a job in such a poor area, but there were places away from communities where Baker could mine. Because those sites would have required the expense of cutting a road or decreasing Baker's profit in some way he refused to consider them. The bumper sticker on his Bronco said it all: Silt Happens.

Many residents had a cousin or an uncle who worked for one of Baker's dozens of businesses. Everyone knew a story about someone Baker had fired for the transgressions of their relatives. Baker was an Anglo, but he was born in Española and had the status of "patrón," a wealthy, powerful man who dispenses favors in exchange for life-long loyalty.

The Anglos who had come to the area had no such fealty. Some came with activist backgrounds. Rose and her family had lived there more than twenty years and had become highly respected citizens because of her work to preserve the local chapel and community traditions. Red-haired, Irish, and Catholic, no way would Rose sit back and let Baker destroy her village.

At the first meeting about the mine Anglos and Hispanos gathered in Rose's living room to address the issue. The village patriarch, who was in his nineties, came and participated although he could not hear well. Everyone in the community revered him and valued his support. Four families, including Rose's, were going to file a lawsuit on the grounds that the mine was a "nuisance," a tepid legal term for actions that might dramatically impact lives. Baker's mine was a threat, not a nuisance.

Rose and others distributed petitions, information about the mine, and addresses and phone numbers of politicians to call or write. We began collecting money to cover expenses like printing and to help with legal costs. I went to hearings in courtrooms in Santa Fe, gathered signatures, and tried to involve others in the struggle. I did not really want to get involved but Rose was very persuasive and I had long-standing activist inclinations. My grandmother belonged to the Women's Christian Temperance Union and was a suffragette who fought for women's right to vote in the early twentieth century. As a high school teacher in the late 1960s I had organized an ecology club and then helped found a chapter of Zero Population Growth in Claremont in the seventies. I helped start a Green Party group in the late eighties.

Baker's lawyers found various ways to keep his mine open and the trucks rolling. Because our group, called Amigos de la Tierra, had little in the way of financial resources closing the mine began to seem less and less possible, but those most affected by the mine refused to give up. Some of the residents devoted nearly all their time to the fray. For weeks one woman with an asthmatic child and an organic farm camped out daily from 8:00 a.m. until 5:00 p.m. at Pete Rahn's office, trying to get enforcement of truck speed and load limits on the road.

Rose had devoted years to developing good rapport with neighbors in San Juan Pueblo. Part of SR 582 that the gravel trucks used runs through the pueblo. The mine also affected residents there. Rose gently lobbied friends in the pueblo to support our efforts. There was scant evidence that Rose's work was having any impact, but everything changed about a year after the mining began. Out of the blue San Juan Pueblo exercised its muscle as a sovereign nation and closed the portion of the road they owned to trucks weighing more than fourteen tons. Running lighter weight trucks was not profitable, Baker said. For once, George Baker was stopped in his tracks.

Katherine Wells

Amigos de la Tierra enjoyed a respite, but members agreed that the area needed an environmental watchdog group. Our mission was to protect traditional agricultural communities, maintain a healthy environment, and protect local archaeological and cultural resources. We reorganized and changed our name to Vecinos del Rio. Rose succeeded in getting the small chapel in her neighborhood placed on the State Register of Cultural Properties and helped to instill pride in the young people of her village about their culture and community. Rose and Hispanos whose families had been in the area for several generations worked to reinvigorate long-standing agricultural practices such as the acequia system and local food production. They interviewed community elders and worked with citizens to mount an exhibit of old photos and documents about the village's history in their chapel.

Though his mine was closed we all knew that George Baker would not give up. He would do whatever he had to do in order to continue mining.

In early 1995 another blow came. We learned that Baker had purchased six thousand acres of land on the mesa that included most of its eastern flank. He already owned much of the mesa top. He had the inside track on local real estate. No one else knew the property was for sale. Baker was the only person in the Española area rich enough to buy the whole tract. I suspected he bought the land for a proverbial song. The land had little potential for development because there was no water and the soil was poor, but it could be mined for rock. The only good news was that virtually all of Baker's new land was too high above the river to have good gravel deposits, so we didn't have to worry about more gravel mines.

The news of his purchase made me feel sick. Now he probably owned 7,500 acres of the mesa and no one knew Baker's intentions. He owned not only a large part of the mesa, but vast archaeological resources. After the second Rock Art Field School recording program on our land in 1994, Jay and Helen Crotty reported that there were more than six thousand petroglyphs on the 188 acres that Lloyd and I owned. Though the concentration of rock art was not as dense on Baker's vast tract, I suspected that there had to be at least twice as many glyphs and other archaeological features on his property as ours. Except for a few spectacular glyphs I doubted that he was aware of his treasures. As far as anyone knew they meant little to him.

I began to receive requests from organizations and individuals for tours of the site after we had lived there a couple of years. I enjoyed sharing the images with other petroglyph enthusiasts. Some had expertise I learned from. A few were famous. Seeing the name of Lucy Lippard on one tour list amazed me. She is a writer and highly influential thinker in the realm of visual art and has long been one of my heroes. A couple of Lucy's books have been very important to my development as an artist. We became friends and fellow rock art adventurers.

One of the most memorable visitors was Ed Krupp, director of the Griffith Observatory in Los Angeles. He came with Von Del Chamberlain, another astronomer from the Salt Lake City planetarium. They are both avid archaeoastronomers interested in petroglyphs of celestial objects. Such petroglyphs may have been solar markers made by the early Puebloans. The pair arrived on an August day when the temperature was over one hundred degrees. Ed's attire baffled me: loafers, slacks, short-sleeved white shirt, and a gaudy tie. My perplexity apparently showed. "He always wears a tie," Von Del offered with a shrug. Oh boy, he's going to wilt after fifteen minutes, I thought to myself as we set out.

Five hours later Von Del and I were spent, soaked with sweat, and dragging along behind Ed who leaped cheerfully from boulder to boulder exclaiming enthusiastically about each new petroglyph. He issued a steady stream of hilarious commentary. Ed could easily have been a stand-up comic. At the end of the day his tie was still in place, he was still joking, and I saw no signs of sweat or fatigue. "How does he do that," I asked Von Del, pointing to Ed. Von Del just shook his head.

Around the time of Baker's big land purchase on the mesa I got a call from a man named Bruce who was an art teacher at San Juan Pueblo Day School. Bruce wanted to bring a group of kids from the school to visit the glyphs and draw the images. About twenty of them came one afternoon. I felt nervous giving them introductory information about the site from an archaeological viewpoint. Would anything I told them

Katherine Wells

conflict with "insider" cultural information they knew? Would they be hostile because I owned this land their ancestors called home? Of course not! They were ten-year-olds, gleefully jumping off boulders and yelling to each other to come see this or that cool glyph they'd found. Their antics scared the bejesus out of me, but I enjoyed them immensely.

The kids visited a second time and then used the images they drew as a basis for art projects back in the classroom. Later Bruce arranged a small exhibit of their work in the pueblo. The pueblo's governor spoke and I was invited to give a brief talk about the petroglyphs on the mesa. I hoped the visits would continue but Bruce moved away the following year and nothing more happened.

Bruce also asked if he could bring a group of elders from the pueblo to visit the glyphs. The prospect of meeting them and witnessing their response to the rock art thrilled me. Whatever the elders' reactions, I vowed not to ask intrusive questions. I hoped they would volunteer thoughts and observations. Some of the images, I had learned, might be sacred to the Tewa or contain information not to be divulged to the non-Pueblo world.

Heavy clouds loomed on the day of the group's first visit. Bruce and about fifteen elders, mostly women, came in two vans. We stood under the carport introducing ourselves. My mind raced trying to size up the situation in terms of their ability to navigate rough terrain. Some clearly wouldn't be able to handle much more than a slow walk along the dirt road. Most wore lightweight street shoes poorly suited to rock-hopping and uneven ground.

Rain began to fall just as we set off on our excursion. The elders laughed, deemed the moisture a blessing, and ducked back under the carport. Now what? I thought. I did the obvious and invited them all into my small living room. Bruce and I quickly arranged some kind of seating for everyone and I put on water for tea.

Rain continued steadily. I brought out a stack of about a hundred photographs of petroglyphs and began passing them around. Some in the group commented on them among themselves with wonder or puzzlement in their soft voices. After serving tea and cookies I sat quietly next to a woman who peered carefully at each photo. After a while she began asking me what various images were. What's wrong with this

Shield image that has the appearance of both a compass and a classic Puebloan four-pointed star. Possible feathers on the edges.

picture? I thought. What an odd feeling to have a Pueblo elder ask me to identify petroglyph images.

I later learned from Wilbur Atencio, an elder and former governor of San Juan Pueblo, that most of the people in the pueblo had never seen the petroglyphs in the area. Wilbur himself knew nothing of them until thirty years earlier when he had walked up the road along the foot of the mesa with his kids picking mulberries. The images on the boulders became more numerous as he walked north and were a revelation to him. When he was young, Wilbur told me, members of the tribe seldom ventured off their small reservation to the wider world that had

　　　　　　　　　　　　　Katherine Wells

been occupied by their Puebloan ancestors. Centuries of oppression by Spanish, then Anglo conquerors kept them close to home.

When the rain stopped the elders piled back into the vans. All seemed genuinely grateful for the experience and wanted to come back when they could walk around and have a closer look at the glyphs.

Later, while discussing the visit and my perplexity about the elders' lack of knowledge to a rock art scholar friend, I began to understand more. "Imagine taking an average contemporary Frenchman into Notre Dame and asking him to identify and explain the host of Christian saints and symbols there," he said. "He couldn't tell you much." A good analogy. Most of the Pueblo IV images were four to seven hundred years old. Many were ancient images few of the present-day Pueblo people had ever seen.

On the elders' second visit a month later we walked carefully along the rutted dirt road and visited easily accessible glyphs. Some of the women brought cornmeal to "feed" the images and offered prayers. The glyphs had been so long without food, they said. Tears crept to my eyes as one of the women sprinkled cornmeal over the sun-headed figure I so loved. I felt honored to be allowed to witness her act.

One of the elders was the mother of San Juan Pueblo's current governor. Her father had brought her to visit the petroglyphs when she was a small child. He had spoken to her about some of the images. "But I don't remember much," she lamented. "You know how kids are. They don't listen." She chuckled softly, then fell silent.

As we headed back to the vans a woman with dark bronze skin walking beside me related that she had just returned to the Pueblo after a couple of decades in California. I told her I had lived there for decades as well. "I'm mostly Indian," she offered. "And a little bit Irish."

"That's funny," I replied. "I'm mostly Irish and a little bit Indian." I visualized our family trees with branches angling in odd convolutions. Our cultural backgrounds and appearances were quite different, but at the level of blood, bone, gene, the difference was academic.

After Lloyd returned from sailing the boat to Mexico in the spring of 1996 he made an appointment with a local urologist because he'd been having a problem with frequent urination. Lloyd had undergone bowel resection surgery when he was in his forties and a recent hernia procedure. Aside from that he had enjoyed robust health all his life. Dr. Frazier ordered the usual prostate tests and announced that Lloyd had a tumor. When he came home Lloyd casually mentioned that he had some kind of problem he would need to address when he returned from his next trip to Mexico in late July. He seemed unconcerned. Perhaps he felt protected by the fact that no one in his family had ever had cancer of any kind. Either Lloyd misunderstood Frazier's first announcement, or he refused to accept it. I knew nothing about prostate problems and didn't think much about what he said.

After the next trip to Mexico Lloyd had another test. I went with him to the doctor's office to talk about the results. It was Friday afternoon. Dr. Frazier said in a solemn voice that Lloyd had a tumor that needed to be dealt with immediately. "It's benign, isn't it?" I blurted. The doctor looked at me over his reading glasses and shook his head. Frazier stated that there are no benign prostate tumors.

Lloyd's prostate specific antigen (PSA) score before he went to Mexico was several points above normal—according to Dr. Frazier, it was about the score when a man should begin some type of treatment. Almost two months passed between the first and second tests. Now his score was much higher. Frazier suggested that Lloyd have a surgery that he likened to a "roto-rooter" process the following Thursday. Lloyd asked if waiting awhile to see how things went was a reasonable option. "You've got to do something," Frazier replied. Lloyd scheduled the surgery.

We left Frazier's office and sat in the car holding hands, frozen in disbelief. Like a mammoth wave breaking over us, the cold, hard weight of cancer began to pull us under. I wondered how far we could swim, how many breaths Lloyd had left. The veins in his forearm stood out as they always did carrying their freight of blood. How long before that freight turned deadly? Lloyd's body was now the enemy.

My feelings were torn between anger, compassion, and fear. I was angry at Lloyd because he had not gone to the doctor sooner, because he had not postponed the boat trip and taken Frazier's original pronouncement seriously. I could tell from the stricken look on Lloyd's face that he was blaming himself for his plight, for pushing his luck. The awful knowledge that delayed treatment might cost him his life had struck.

The future had all the allure of a minefield.

Lloyd expressed a strong aversion to Frazier. I thought he was "shooting the messenger," but supported his decision to seek a second opinion. Finding another urologist who could see him before the scheduled surgery would be difficult. We arrived home at 5:00 p.m., too late to make any calls.

On Saturday we went on a hike a few miles away on land owned by the Bureau of Land Management that was supposed to have a lot of interesting petroglyphs I had never seen. Any other time our discoveries would have delighted me, but every moment was dulled by the painful knowledge Lloyd and I were trying to digest. Cancer walked with us, an unshakable presence that colored everything. The monster was in the car, the house, the air. We ate and slept and bathed with it. We didn't talk about "it" very much, but it was everywhere. I knew the dragging hours were worse for Lloyd than for me. We both needed time to process this new reality and come to terms with the beast. Every thought of what lay ahead ended in an abyss. We needed information to help understand this razor-strewn terrain.

Saturday night we went to a movie in Santa Fe and it was a welcome distraction. Sunday we hiked up the road with the dogs. Shaggy Dog had died a year before and been replaced by Zeus, a good-natured German shepherd mix I adopted from the Española animal shelter because Ginger was so distraught by Shaggy Dog's absence. Ginger regarded Zeus with contempt even though he outweighed her by twenty-five pounds. In her eyes he was a sorry substitute for Shaggy Dog. Zeus willingly let Ginger be the alpha dog. I suspected Zeus had been mistreated in the past because he cowered when anyone made an abrupt move near him. In time he grew more relaxed in spite of Ginger's haughty attitude.

On our hike my spirits lifted a little. The beauty of the cumulus clouds over the Sangres, the sky's Tiepolo blue hue, the comforting, familiar boulders and hills, felt reassuring. Lloyd and I sat in the meager shade of a big juniper to rest. The dogs took refuge from the late August heat under the tree's low branches. We gave them water in a plastic margarine tub I carried in my backpack. Lloyd and I both smiled at the heartwarming sound of dogs lapping water.

On Monday Lloyd called three or four urologists in Santa Fe and found one that had an opening on Wednesday. We sat in his office hardly breathing as Dr. Milton read the test reports Lloyd had brought along. "I can see no reason to recommend the surgery you have scheduled," he stated. He said that type of surgery was seldom used anymore and that it seemed inappropriate in Lloyd's case. Lloyd heaved a monumental sigh of relief. He called to cancel the surgery from Santa Fe.

Dr. Milton discussed the idea of prostate removal with Lloyd, but clarified that the cancer was already outside the prostate "capsule" and therefore incurable. He started Lloyd on a drug that he thought would slow the cancer's growth and put him on the hospital's schedule for radiation beginning in mid-November. Dr. Milton recommended a couple of books to read to educate ourselves about the disease and suggested some supplements Lloyd should consider taking. He set a follow-up appointment for a few weeks later.

We asked the doctor about Lloyd's prognosis. As expected he was vague, but thought Lloyd had a few to several years depending on. . . . The "depending on" list was long: how Lloyd responded to radiation and the drug Dr. Milton gave him; whether or not the cancer traveled to his bones or lymph nodes; whether he would need chemotherapy and how much; how aggressive the cancer turned out to be.

We ordered a couple of books and began to learn about the disease. Not only was prostate cancer complex, the number of variables at any stage made determining what to expect difficult to impossible. There are a maddening number of schools of thought about conventional and alternative treatment and approaches. Lloyd and I both felt as though we were entering a wilderness without a compass or any survival tools.

After we had a couple of weeks to adjust to the reality of cancer in our lives Lloyd and I revisited our house-building plans. The decision about whether or not to go ahead and build loomed. If we built both of us agreed that we should again use straw bales for construction. The small house required very little heat in winter and minimal cooling in summer. The thick walls acted as a perfect sound barrier. Lloyd and I were absolutely sold on the material after living in the small house for a few seasons.

Katherine Wells

In late 1993, Lloyd and I had been proud to be represented in the first substantial volume published about the straw-bale building phenomenon. We were contacted by Bill Steen, a photographer, and his wife, Athena Swentzell Steen, a writer and native of Santa Clara Pueblo. Along with straw bale guru David Bainbridge they were writing a book about building with straw. The Steens lived in Tucson, a hotbed of straw-bale construction. They came and photographed both the studio and the small house and asked many questions. Both structures were featured in *The Straw Bale House*, a handsome book published in 1994.

But now I privately questioned the wisdom of building a second house given the uncertainty of the future. On the one hand what would I want with a bigger house if Lloyd were gone? Would I even want to stay here? (Of course I would. How could I leave my petroglyph "babies"?) On the other hand, building might be a good idea because we could rent out the small house as we had originally planned. Building would also provide Lloyd with a project to occupy his mind and use his creative talents. I knew from experience that he needed to be engaged using his hands. After a long, painful discussion, Lloyd and I decided to go ahead and build.

There was another thorny issue for me. Ownership. Though we had not settled firmly on a house site Lloyd and I agreed that the structure should be on one of the two parcels of land we owned jointly. I hoped Lloyd had many years of life left, but I felt I had to face the property issue now. If we built as co-owners and Lloyd died, where would that leave me? Understandably Lloyd would want his six children to inherit his assets when he died. If we owned the house and land together then I would have to buy his children out. What worried me was that Lloyd's second wife, Marcy, could be difficult. I feared she would be on my doorstep the moment Lloyd was gone trying to manipulate the situation. I had seen a couple of appalling demonstrations of Marcy's guile since Lloyd and I had been together. I wanted no part of her. Since the manifestations of Lloyd's cancer were still minimal, grappling with such issues seemed strange, but neither of us could deny the reality of the diagnosis. I also wanted to be the person to decide what would happen to the land and the petroglyphs. I did not want to risk having anybody else involved in that decision.

The only thing I could think of to do, if he was willing, if I could manage it, was to buy Lloyd out and finance the building of the house myself. The value of the property had appreciated quite a bit in the few years since our purchase. I would have to make Lloyd an offer based on current real-estate prices. I spent a few days going over my finances, figuring and refiguring. There was enough risk involved to make me nervous, but I decided that buying Lloyd out was the right thing to do.

I drew up a proposal and presented it to Lloyd. He didn't like the idea of building "my house" or living in "my house" again, but he understood my point of view. Lloyd also realized that selling his interest in the property would give him more financial flexibility. He thought about the proposition for a couple of days and decided to accept my offer.

Lloyd had been working on house drawings now and then for a year or so. He had come up with a rough plan that we both liked. We were in general agreement about the structure's size, shape, and other basic features. We agreed that the house should be Pueblo style to blend in with the landscape and local architecture.

Initially Lloyd favored building on a site about a fifteen-minute walk from the trailer. I convinced him the best spot was where the Silver Streak sat. We already had a road, power, and a well there. Developing a road and the utilities for the other location would have been a large, costly endeavor. And the studio was close to the Streak. I didn't want to have to hike or drive back and forth to the studio. The real clincher for me, though, was that the site of the trailer was in the midst of the largest concentration of petroglyphs on the property and near the ones that were the most vulnerable to vandalism. As their protector I felt like I needed to be there.

We wanted to minimize the disturbance of the land as much as possible. To maximize our beloved view of the Sangre de Cristos and the river valley we decided that the living/dining/kitchen area should be oriented to that view. The bedroom and office end of the house would be oriented for the greatest passive solar gain in winter. Lloyd modified our plan and produced a pleasing shallow chevron-shaped building that would require only a minor amount of alteration to the land. The guest room on the back of the house would be on a slightly higher level, which would create more interesting lines on the building's exterior and help minimize the amount of cutting required. Our landscaping would be the artfully arranged boulders and native grasses and cacti that were already there. We wanted the house to be somewhat rustic, but elegant, simple and solid in feeling.

Even though we had already built the studio and small house, I had some misgivings about building our "dream house" on the land because the site was so sacred to Native Americans. This felt different. This was putting down roots. I was keenly aware that I was imposing my house on somebody else's history. On reflection I realized that every house I had ever lived in was built on Indian land. The difference was that here, I was breaking the ground.

Lloyd and I talked about how much time and energy he wanted to devote to the construction of the house given his health and other issues, like the boat. We met with Ernie, a contractor from the area. We had visited a couple of houses he built and Lloyd was impressed with Ernie's workmanship. Ernie had no experience with straw-bale construction but was interested in working with the material. Since Lloyd and I had two straw buildings under our belts and knew the medium to be forgiving and low-tech, Ernie's inexperience didn't concern us. Common sense and guidance from Lloyd should forestall major problems. Ernie looked at our provisional plans. After some discussion he was satisfied that he could handle the job. We told him about Lloyd's health. He was willing to have Lloyd be part of the work crew as much as he wanted to. We agreed to meet again in a month.

Eight

I regarded my hours in the studio as mental-health time. I was suspended in the electric flow of energy from my heart/brain to my hands. Sometimes I had to stop and use my critical faculties to assess what should come next or to solve a problem, but for the most part answers came intuitively. Being in that "flow" is a Himalayan high. Usually I am happy with the "products," but the process is a slice of Nirvana.

Getting myself established as an artist in New Mexico required a lot of work and expense visiting galleries, sending out information about my work, having each piece professionally photographed, and learning who's who in the New Mexico art world in 1995. I had met a woman who belonged to a group of women artists that met monthly for lunch. They invited me to join. I came to enjoy their company and learned a lot about various galleries and the "players" in the local art world.

Images I had created of Our Lady of Guadalupe filled the walls and worktable in my studio. Since my first tentative steps in 1994 I had produced more than twenty nontraditional images of Guadalupe in all sizes and guises. Many involved the use of bullets. One is a three-foot-high

Nuestra Señora de la Sangre de los Niños. Mixed-media triptych
sculpture, 36" x 25" x 3". In private collection. Photo by the author.

Katherine Wells

freestanding triptych featuring three figures of the virgin, two of them holding long bullets as though they were candles. The central figure clutches the Christ Child to her chest. Narrow lines of text along the edges of each panel name gun brands and the title of the piece: *Nuestra Señora de la Sangre de los Niños*. I made regular trips to a target-shooting range in Santa Fe to buy spent shell casings and slugs to fit them. "What do you do with all these?" the clerk asked after my third visit. "Crafts project," I replied, heading for the door. Since he worked in a store that sold guns I suspected he would not be receptive to my opinions about gun violence in our country.

In another sculpture Guadalupe appears against a collaged background of hundred-dollar bills. She holds a rolled piece of currency in her hands. Her title is *Nuestra Señora de los Dólares*, a play on the Spanish word "dolor," which means sorrow or pain, and the word "dolar," the Spanish version of the word "dollar."

In one of my favorite pieces I dressed her in the American flag and gave her a small Mexican flag to hold with the title *The Undocumented Virgin*. She has definitely crossed the border along with millions of her illegal alien countrymen.

The work sold readily. I showed several small images of Guadalupe at Talley Richards's gallery in Taos. In one the figure hugs a bullet to her chest. One day a local developmentally disabled man came into the gallery to look around. Taoseños looked after him. Talley greeted him warmly. He glanced around and walked over to the image, pausing to study it. After a couple of minutes Talley asked him to comment on the piece. "She's keeping the bullets out of the guns," he said. The story gave me goose bumps. I wished I had been able to articulate the work's meaning half as well.

My magnum opus is a figure four feet high whose arms and robe open out to reveal a niche inside. The cave-like space houses a skeletal figure wearing a skirt made of braided snakes. Small skulls surrounded her. The piece is my homage to the Aztec goddess Coatlicúe, a predecessor of Guadalupe's who embodied the inseparable powers of creation and destruction, birth and death, the ultimate power of nature. Christianity has given short shrift to that reality and I liked the fact that she is part of Guadalupe's "baggage." I titled the piece *La Guadalupana Azteca*.

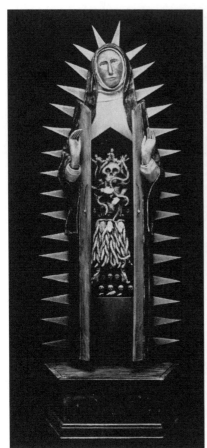

Left: *La Guadalupana Azteca*, a mixed-media nicho sculpture figure
that opens to reveal the Aztec goddess Coatlicúe, 47" x 16" x 7".
In private collection. **Right:** Controversial *Barbielupe*, mixed-media sculpture,
12" x 5" x 3". Photos by Pat Pollard.

The Guadalupe image I created that ultimately received the most
attention is *Barbielupe*. I used a regular Barbie doll and changed her
arms so that her hands were folded in front of her chest in a prayerful
attitude. I made her a rose-colored dress and a blue robe to go over it.
Tiny golden rays surround the figure. Her beautiful blond hair cascades
out of the robe onto her shoulder. I intended to acknowledge Barbie as
the patron saint of little girls, but more importantly, I wanted to call

Katherine Wells

attention to our culture's worship of female thinness. The number of teenage girls who die annually from anorexia horrifies me. The point of the piece is that Guadalupe, as a representative of the feminine in the world, would be horrified. Those who understood the image loved it. Those who did not screamed blasphemy.

I had my first solo exhibit in New Mexico in 1996 at Hand Artes Gallery in Truchas. Most of the pieces in the show were images of Guadalupe. *La Guadalupana Azteca* sold before the opening reception to a woman who was a Jungian analyst in Berkeley. Perfect, I thought, though I was loath to let the piece go.

That year I also showed work in galleries in Albuquerque and Taos and in an exhibit at the state capitol building in Santa Fe. In the summer an artist friend invited me to exhibit with three other women at the desanctified Santuario of Guadalupe in Santa Fe, which had been the first church in New Mexico dedicated to Our Lady of Guadalupe. The space is now used for concerts, lectures, and musical events. I exhibited several of my nontraditional images of Guadalupe, wondering if the Catholic manager of the space who was on the board of directors of the Santuario would object. He didn't say a word then, but four years later he was among those who demanded the removal of my work from the space.

In 2000, I exhibited *Barbielupe* and other pieces in another exhibit at the Santuario. The board of directors ordered me to remove my work even though I had shown similar work there before without objection. As a result I ended up with my work on the front page of the *Santa Fe New Mexican* in color. I became part of a large and furious uproar between angry conservative Catholics and the Museum of New Mexico about "appropriate" images of Guadalupe. The next year, Alma López, a Mexican artist who lives in California and created an image of Guadalupe in a so-called bikini, received ugly threats when her work was exhibited at the Museum of International Folk Art in Santa Fe. So did museum officials. Later on a scholar writing her PhD dissertation on contemporary images of the Virgin made great use of my work in her writing.

In the fall Lloyd and I tackled the utility projects that had to be addressed before the house could be built. We went through the permitting process, then hired a local company to install the septic tank and leach field across the driveway from the studio. We moved the trailer to a spot near the dirt road, then ran the power and phone lines under the driveway to the nearest utility pole. We hired Pablo and his cousin Freddie to help with the work. While we were at it we ran power, water, septic system pipes, and phone lines to the trailer, which we had rented out after we moved into the first house. That way we could continue to rent out the Streak until we were ready to sell it.

All autumn we continued to refine the house plans. With the trailer moved Lloyd was able to start surveying the house site with a transit to calculate how much cut and fill work would be required.

One morning in late October I was helping Lloyd with surveying work by holding the "story pole" while he took readings with the transit. We heard what sounded like a large truck coming up the road. I turned to see a shiny red eighteen-wheel side-dump truck heading up the mesa. What the hell is this about, I wondered. George Baker had not hauled any rock off the mesa for a couple of years. Another identical truck followed five minutes later. Oh God, I thought. An hour later the trucks came back down the road filled with rocks from Baker's stockpile near the large Awanyu petroglyph. They returned in the afternoon and loaded up again. The same trucks came and went often in the following weeks. I stopped one of the trucks one day and asked the driver what they were up to. "Just hauling rock, ma'am," he answered. He said he didn't know how long it would go on, but the hauling ceased after the first part of December.

In early November I went to the boat with Lloyd. The vessel was now in La Paz, Mexico, on the Sea of Cortez. When we returned he would begin radiation treatments. A couple of days after our arrival in Mexico we were joined by Lloyd's oldest daughter, Michele, and her partner Rick. I knew Michele better than any of Lloyd's other children. We got along well. In time I came to love her as a daughter. She is a film producer, an exceptionally bright, energetic, and compassionate person. The four of us spent a couple of days exploring La Paz. I tried every available flavor of exotic tropical ice cream: guava, papaya, coconut, mango, tamarindo. Then we sailed the boat to a small island nearby. We spent lazy days strolling beaches we had all to ourselves, visiting coves filled with pelicans in our Zodiac dinghy, and being dazzled by the surreal turquoise hues of the Sea of Cortez with our eyes. The gentle waves lapping against the boat lulled us like babies. A sweet time for all of us.

Back home I accompanied Lloyd to the cold steel, tile, and sterility of St. Vincent's Hospital; to a cold machine and searing beams we hoped would tame his cancer, even if it could not be killed. Lloyd drove to Santa Fe for treatments five days a week for six weeks. The process tired him, but he insisted on driving himself every time. "I think if I only had two hours to live I could drive for one of them," he told me. The man had a mountain of grit he used to pave the road cancer dragged him down.

In December Lloyd and I began to second-guess our decision to build the house. The design was much more complex and the building process would be more complicated than the small house or the studio. Did we really know what we were doing? Was the plan we had developed the best arrangement for the way we lived? Would it be a house somebody else would buy if we ever had to sell? We stewed together and separately. I had a lot of confidence in Lloyd's judgment. His questioning made me nervous.

"How about," I said, "we get an architect to come out and consult with us?" We knew of one in Santa Fe who had designed a couple of straw-bale houses. Lloyd liked the idea. We contacted Phyllis Greer who came out, walked the site, and talked to us for a couple of hours about how we lived and what our tastes were. She asked many questions, trying to get a sense of what kind of plan would suit us best. Greer agreed to do a sketch based on our requirements and the size and shape of the site.

Ten days later we met in her office. The house plan Greer presented had the feel of an attractive, comfortable house, but it wasn't for us. Neither Lloyd nor I liked the way the plan related to the site. Driving home we went over the pros and cons of her plan versus our plan. "Makes me feel good," Lloyd said. We agreed to stick to our plan. We had studied the site for four years, knew the weather patterns, where the sun was any given month, knew our habits. The cost of the consultation was money well spent. Now we had more confidence in our own ideas.

Lloyd bought a bag of red pottery clay and made hundreds of tiny bricks on the scale of a straw bale. He dried them in the sun, then built a model of the house on a piece of plywood so that we could really see how the finished house would look in three dimensions. When Lloyd finished we carried the model outside and oriented it in the same direction the house would sit. We checked the model frequently, noting how the light moved at various times of the day. I even made cardboard furniture to scale to get an idea of how to furnish the house. All I needed were some dolls to be back in my childhood.

After Lloyd's radiation treatments ended in mid-December he had another PSA test. We got the results after Christmas. His score was on the low end of the normal range. He would need to be retested every three months. We were hopeful that the scores would remain low. The year 1997 started on a bright note.

In mid-January Lloyd went to Baja for a couple of weeks. When he was gone I had more time in the studio and the leisure to enjoy hiking the mesa. January and February had many sparkling days with temperatures as high as sixty degrees. My idea of perfect. Now and then I revisited the giant Awanyu and the life-sized upside-down figure on what was now George Baker's property. There were no "no trespassing" signs so I continued to explore his land, as did many of my neighbors. I visited a long arroyo that was partly on his land and partly on mine that had hundreds of glyphs, including outstanding shield bearers and a rock traversed by about a dozen two-inch-long carved footprints. On my section of the arroyo was a ten-foot-wide boulder covered with images including four connected spirals I would have sworn were Celtic and a Zia symbol similar to the one on the New Mexico state flag.

In a remote arroyo on Baker's land I discovered a life-sized image of a human wearing a headdress shaped like a stepped cloud terrace. The carefully carved glyph differed stylistically from everything else I had seen on the mesa. Given its location and deep repatination I suspected that less than a handful of humans had seen the image in the last four hundred years. The thrilling find made me appreciate all over again my good fortune at being in such a unique place. I sat with the boulder in the winter sun trying to teleport my mind to the time of its creation.

Around a large, open meadow far from the river on Baker's land I

Straw bales for house on a truck. The Sangre de Cristo Mountains in the background. Photo by the author.

found dozens of odd Historic period images. Some seemed like misguided renditions of older motifs and themes. Because of the glyphs' location I conjectured that the area might have been a place of refuge before or after the Pueblo Revolt of 1680. Perhaps Pueblo people fled there when the repressive practices of the conquerors became intolerable. To me there seemed to be a disconnect between the Historic rock art there and elsewhere on the mesa.

The dogs and I relished our explorations in the crisp winter air. From the mesa top I could see the snow-covered Sangres, Taos Mountain, the Jemez Mountains, and even the Sandias above Albuquerque. My God, my God, I exclaimed over and over, reveling in the beauty before me. Such transcendent moments on the face of our tender planet! After almost five years on the mesa I was still perpetually in awe of my surroundings and my good fortune to live in such a place.

When Lloyd returned from Baja we began to focus on the new house.

The contractor, Ernie, was on another job until April. Lloyd felt strong and decided to go ahead with the preliminary work for the footings, ordering the straw and lumber, working out the configuration of the tubing for the radiant floor heating system, and other important tasks. We met with the plumber and the electrician Ernie had chosen for the job.

In early February George Baker's trucks reappeared on the road. This time not just two trucks, but ten or twelve monster eighteen-wheelers rumbled up the road starting at daylight. They went back down loaded with rock they hauled to somewhere unknown and then returned for another load of stone. The behemoths worked sporadically at first, but the number of loads soon increased until they were groaning up and down all day followed by heavy clouds of dust they kicked up from the road. Alarm bells in my head reached high decibels when a huge machine went up the road with an attachment about three-feet-long that looked like a giant steel pencil. I had no idea what the monster was until I heard the sickening sound of breaking rock. The trucks woke us every morning as they came up the road. Our bedroom windows in the small house were only fifty or sixty feet from the road. Only the dead could sleep through the din.

Neighbors and members of Vecinos del Rio had been calling for weeks wanting to know what was going on. People a mile or more away could hear the sound and were alarmed. Baker had quickly hauled off the huge stockpiles of boulders in the meadow below the big Awanyu. He was mining and hauling six days a week and his trucks were zipping through the neighborhood well above the speed limit. Bulldozers now assaulted the hillside opposite the big serpent petroglyph, ripping out rocks as big as eight- or ten-feet across. The rock-breaking machine reduced them to smaller sizes. My horror level increased tenfold. What if Baker kept doing this for years? Would he mine the other side of the little valley where the Awanyu is? Could anybody stop him? Where was the rock going? Can I live here if he's going to mine forever? Suddenly I had regrets about having purchased Lloyd's share of our land. Baker began mining in another area as well—this one on my property boundary. The sound of the machinery made me grit my teeth all day.

Over a period of a few weeks my New Mexico haven morphed into a rock mining hell. For a while I felt mentally paralyzed. I had learned enough about George Baker to know that having a conversation with him, if that were possible, would be a waste of breath. He did what he wanted on his own terms and considered what he called "newcomers," people like me, worthless troublemakers.

I felt intimidated. When Vecinos del Rio fought against his mine some of Baker's truckers harassed the more vocal members of the community who protested. I'm a sitting duck, I thought. Since we have no close neighbors I felt vulnerable. Lloyd hated what Baker was doing, but kept out of the situation emotionally. I couldn't. Baker was threatening my home, my petroglyphs, his petroglyphs, and my sanity.

Nearly every day there was a close call between one of Baker's trucks and me, Lloyd, or one of the guys working on the house. Our dirt road is a single lane. A car or a pickup cannot pass an eighteen-wheeler. There is one nasty blind curve where meeting a truck going downhill while you are going up is more than hair-raising. One has to back down the rough, steep road to allow the truck to pass. More than once I panicked as I faced forty tons of truck and rock bearing down on me.

In spite of my fear I began to think of ways to thwart Baker. I knew he was breaking the law by hauling seventy-five to eighty thousand pounds on SR 582 at the bottom of my hill every day. Though narrow and twisting the road was a state highway and clearly posted with a fourteen-ton load limit. Several of my neighbors, members of Vecinos del Rio, and I had been calling NMDOT daily for weeks trying to get the load limit enforced. Nothing happened. Baker was a good friend of the higher ups in the department.

I wanted to know if Baker was violating other statutes. After talking to neighbors and members of Vecinos del Rio I concluded that he was probably selling the rock to the Bureau of Reclamation (BOR). Using an alias I called their Albuquerque office to find out. No, the underling I spoke to said. Baker was hauling riprap for them from an area south of Santa Fe, but not in my neighborhood. I didn't believe it. There are few customers for such large quantities of riprap—all big government agencies. I checked with the Corps of Engineers. They also denied having a contract with Baker.

I thought there must be some regulation against the mining because of the archaeological treasures in the area. However, I knew that in general there is no protection for rock art on private land. If Baker wanted to sell his petroglyphs to Joe Blow he could do so. He could even grind them into gravel. I had learned from the State Historic Preservation Office (SHPO) that this was true not only in New Mexico, but everywhere in the United States. The only items of Native American culture that are protected on private property are graves and grave goods. Even that level of protection is recent.

The third time I called the Bureau of Reclamation I spoke with a man named Art Valverde who admitted that much to his surprise he had discovered that Baker was hauling some stockpiled rock from the mesa for BOR. "The stockpile is gone," I said. "He's mining! I can hear it all day every day. I've seen the machinery."

"Only stockpiled rock," he repeated. I hung up. I got the feeling BOR either didn't know or didn't want to know what Baker was doing. I had read *Cadillac Desert*, which I think should be required reading for everyone who lives west of the Rocky Mountains. The book made clear how monolithic and unmovable the bureaucracy of any agency is. Might as well try to fight God, I thought.

Around the end of March I decided to consult a real-estate lawyer about Baker's easement rights on the dirt road. For a recommendation I called the law firm that had helped me write my will. They said Len Hassett was the best around. Len was more relaxed than most lawyers I had met and had a good sense of humor. I sat in his office and described the situation I was faced with. "What's the name of the guy doing the mining?" he asked.

"Baker," I replied. Hassett threw his head back and laughed.

"It ain't funny," I said. Len apologized and explained that he knew of countless cases where individuals and government agencies at various levels had tried to bring Baker to heel with little success. He had a long list of fines and citations that read like a criminal rap sheet. Apparently to Baker such annoyances were just part of the cost of doing business. Len and I discussed the legal points in my situation. He gave me a copy of a statute that showed Baker was in clear violation of easement law because his hauling on the road vastly exceeded any prior use he had made of it. Hassett said I could sue Baker if I wanted and would probably win, but would have no power to get the judgment enforced. He stressed that Baker could clean me out financially with countersuits.

"Never, ever get into court with Baker," Len admonished. The take-home message was that in rural New Mexico a patrón like Baker could do whatever he wanted.

"Tradition supercedes law," Lloyd summarized when I told him about my visit with Hassett. The reality of that truth was bitter to learn, but at least now I knew the lay of the land.

In early April I went on a trip to some extraordinary petroglyph sites in Arizona with three rock art friends. I went with my friend Sandra, who drove my car. I expressed my fears and frustrations about Baker and building the house. I had already spent more than $15,000 and expenditures were about to mount exponentially with the pouring of the concrete slab and all the materials and labor costs coming up in the next couple of months. Was I about to spend a couple hundred thousand dollars on a house I couldn't stand to live in if Baker kept mining? Who would want to live there? What would the property be worth? Others who lived along the road were also worried about property values declining. I was beginning to think that Lloyd was right about building on one of our parcels of land to the south. At least there we would not have trucks so close to the house.

I was concerned that the constant vibration from eighteen-wheeler trucks was endangering my petroglyphs. Many rocks with glyphs are on precarious slopes close to the road. How many passing loaded trucks would it take to dislodge them? I also worried about a downhill truck going over the edge on the steepest section of the road if its brakes failed. Many glyphs could be destroyed in addition to damage to truck and driver. There were many possibilities for disaster. Sandra counseled me to stop the house project and wait a year or two and see what happened; to cut my losses before they mounted any higher. Sandra's advice went round and round in my head.

Back home I pondered the 650 straw bales that had been delivered in February. They were stacked in the driveway waiting to become a house. I walked around my $3,000 pile of lumber that would become posts, window bucks, doorframes, bond beam, and decking. I climbed

The devastation of Baker's boulder mine in an
archaeologically sensitive area. Photo by the author.

up to the Key Rock and sat with my back against the stone's warm surface. A few spring wildflowers bloomed around me. I plucked a small,
bright yellow, daisylike blossom. The fact that such vibrant color could
spring from poor arid and stony soil buoyed my spirits. I took a deep
breath and decided to fight.

I jolted awake at the sound of the first truck struggling up the hill. The
blurry blue numbers on the clock said 5:02 a.m. The trucks came earlier
and earlier as spring days lengthened. As trucks went up the mesa they
assaulted us with the sound of the struggling engines on the steep grades
below the small house and above the new house site. When they came
down we were assaulted by the sound of Jake brakes blaring so loudly

neighbors could hear them a mile away. Lloyd and I had stopped a couple of truckers and asked them to tell other drivers not to use their Jake brakes but two of the drivers continued, apparently just to harass us.

In addition to waking us ever earlier the constant passage of trucks caused clouds of dust to hang in the dry air all day. We called Baker's compliance officer and requested water trucks to dampen the dust but none came. I found out from NMDOT that the rock trucks were supposed to be tarped, but Baker was violating that rule as well. On one occasion an eighteen-inch rock fell off a truck on a curve on the paved road. One of my neighbors driving behind the truck nearly ran into it.

The speed of the trucks on SR 582 scared the hell out of everyone. The road was posted for forty miles per hour but the truckers invariably drove sixty or more in spite of the curves. The only way they could make any money was to make the maximum number of trips every day.

And a truck killed Domingo. In spite of my two dogs only policy we had adopted the runty dachshund who followed us as we drove up the road one Sunday and made himself at home. Domingo had a patch of bare skin measuring about three-by-eight inches on his back. The hair appeared to have been permanently burned off. Looking at the spot made me cringe, but Domingo seemed oblivious. Another throwaway dog, I thought.

Domingo marched into our lives and instantly became the alpha dog. Big goofy Zeus dutifully marched to his tune, Ginger tolerated him, and Qaddafi the cat seemed mystified, especially when Domingo tried to hump him.

Short as his legs were Domingo loved hiking as much as the other dogs. He bounded over the cactus like a gymnast. I winced every time, fearing his "equipment" would surely be impaled. An invisible magic shield seemed to protect him. Not once did he get stuck.

When the trucks came Domingo would run toward the dirt road and bark at them. He disappeared several months after the hauling began. We couldn't find him anywhere. A couple of days later a neighbor called saying he had found a dog that had been hit by a truck. The neighbor kindly buried Domingo. I was angry with the trucker who hit him and didn't stop, although he may not have known. The huge truck may have drowned out the yelp of a small dog. I was angry with myself for not taking better care of the pup.

The work and stress of house building and trucks and mining and trying to fight Baker and the lack of sleep made me chronically tired. When I went to bed at night my mind kept running all the problems and details of construction, phone conversations I had with people at NMDOT, attempts to get information from the Bureau of Reclamation, and a thousand other things. I tried my best to get to sleep at a reasonable time every night because I knew the trucks would come before daylight. Hurry up and sleep didn't work. My only consolation was that I knew the rest of the neighborhood was awake and angry too. The trucks awakened everyone as they sped through the community. I counted on collective anger as a weapon in the fight against Baker.

In late April the concrete slab for the house had been poured. The pour went well but I was on the verge of abandoning the whole project then and had nearly abandoned it two weeks earlier when we ordered the concrete for the footings. I suffered a moral crisis. I had thought I could avoid buying concrete from George Baker but learned that he owned every concrete batch plant within an hour's drive. "So I'll have it brought up from Albuquerque. I don't care if it costs more," I told Lloyd.

"Won't do," he replied. He explained that concrete that has been in the truck for more than an hour is likely to lose its integrity and cause all kinds of problems in the pour. He had worked with concrete for thirty-five years. There was no arguing with him. If Lloyd was going to have anything to do with the pour the concrete would have to come from Baker. We had decided that our finished floor would be colored cement so the quality of the material during the pour was critical. The idea of putting money in Baker's pocket did not bother Lloyd. For me it was a huge bolus to swallow.

In addition to fatigue I was suffering acutely from dry eye syndrome. I had begun having problems in 1994, but lately the malady had become much worse. I put special drops in my eyes several times a day, applied warm compresses at night, and took vitamin supplements, but experienced little relief. Stress compounded the problem. Sometimes by evening it felt like my eyes were on fire and boatloads of eye drops would not have helped. The surface of my eyes felt like twenty-grit sandpaper.

"How can you stand it?" Lloyd asked, peering at my arid peepers one evening. I shrugged. Kicking back with a warm washcloth over

Katherine Wells

my eyes half the day would make them feel better, but that was not my style. Going back to California might have helped some, but I wasn't ready to throw in the towel. I was wound like an automaton and would drag myself on whatever the cost. Baker had pushed my obsessive-compulsive button.

My neighbors and I continued to try to get NMDOT to enforce the load limit on SR 582. We made call after call to no avail. I had a memorable conversation with one Michael Manning of the department who blithely assured that there were no load limit signs on the road! His assertion left me speechless. After we talked I grabbed my camera and drove down to photograph all four signs. I had duplicate prints made. I wanted one set to send to Mike Manning and another to prove that the signs were there in case they mysteriously disappeared.

My neighbor Leon followed a truck one day to find out exactly where all the rock was going. We knew the trucks went beyond Santa Fe. Leon tailed one all the way to Cochiti and found a huge stockpile of rock accumulating there. Presumably the Bureau of Reclamation would use the rock to shore up the banks of the Rio Grande below Cochiti Dam when they needed it. I wrote letters to the governors of Cochiti and several other pueblos hoping they would be offended that BOR was removing rock from a site sacred to their ancestors, but I received no replies.

Some days I was so preoccupied with Baker's trucks and mining that I paid scant attention to house construction. Ernie had begun working just before the concrete pour. Between him and Lloyd the process was going smoothly. Ernie brought four other guys onto the job. Two were unskilled labor and the others, Ben and Jack, were carpenters. With Lloyd, Pablo, Freddie, and another cousin of Pablo's we had a crew of eight.

After a couple of days I could tell that Jack was going to get on my nerves. He was a highly skilled finish carpenter who lived far out in space mentally and politically. To call him a right-winger doesn't begin to cover it. Jack spun lunatic theories and shared his opinions generously. One of Jack's favorite rants was that the U.S. Navy caused El Niño with some mysterious Tesla technology they practiced out in the middle of the Pacific Ocean. He listened to right-wing radio as though it were broadcast from heaven. I just kept my distance from him as much as possible. Lloyd found Jack amusing.

In early May posts began to rise and the house suddenly had shape. After months of work on the horizontal plane, seeing vertical timbers cheered me up. My elation was short-lived. We had rain off and on for several days that curtailed the work. And crew problems were brewing. One day Jack blew up at something Lloyd said and threw a tantrum to equal any three-year-old's best effort. Lloyd professed not to understand why Jack exploded. The next day they made peace. The episode unnerved me.

A couple of days later Pablo got so angry with Ernie I thought they were going to fight. Pablo accused Ernie of being a racist. Pablo was ugly mad and used vicious, racist language himself, but Ernie stayed under control. I was in the studio trying to focus on an art idea. I seldom had time or energy for creative work at that point but took advantage of spare moments. Pablo and Ernie were just outside. I went out thinking my presence would make them stop. Pablo spewed on. Finally he backed off. I told him to go home. The next day he and Ernie made an uneasy peace, but Pablo was still feeling wounded. I had not seen anything that I would call racist behavior from Ernie.

Two days later Pablo and Freddie quit, partly because they wanted a raise. I didn't think Ernie should be involved so I made the decision. I said no because I didn't see that they merited more money at that point. Freddie and Pablo got in their truck and left. I felt like a failure. Pablo had a chip on his shoulder that got in his way, but I cared about him and wanted to help him mature. I was so exhausted mentally and physically between fighting Baker and the trucks and tending to house construction, all I could do was sit on a straw bale and bawl.

Lloyd jumped out of bed as though he had been shot and started pulling on his jeans. The clock said 3:50 a.m. The first trucks were coming up the road. Lloyd ran out the door and climbed into his car before they rolled past the house. He followed the first two trucks up to the mine in the pitch darkness. The drivers were both kids not much older than twenty. Lloyd dressed them down with all the fury and vitriol of a drill sergeant and told them never, ever to come up the road again before 7:30. The guys mumbled apologies for waking us up and said they just wanted to be first in line to have their trucks loaded so they could make as many round trips back and forth to Cochiti as possible. Lloyd gave them an earful about what they could tell Baker, then came back home and fell asleep. I was as wide-awake as if I were going to my own execution.

For a couple of days the trucks didn't arrive until 5:30 and it seemed like the drivers were trying to be as quiet as possible. No Jake brakes. Then they were back to starting at 4:45. By 6:00 a.m. every day six or eight trucks had already gone up the mesa. My neighbor Jim Edwards and I began videotaping the loaded trucks on SR 582 as proof that they were violating the load limit.

In response to a barrage of calls and letters from Vecinos members and other people who lived along the road the state police came out and stopped a couple of trucks one day, but they had no scales to weigh them. I couldn't see why they needed them. Even when the trucks were empty they approached the fourteen-ton load limit. The police said they would begin patrolling with scales.

Suddenly there were fewer trucks and they ran sporadically. Apparently Baker was playing cat and mouse with the state police. I drove to the post office on the fifth of May and had the pleasure of seeing four trucks pulled over a couple of miles away. NMDOT was weighing the monsters. I wanted to get out of my car and do a little jig while thumbing my nose at the drivers. But it wasn't the truckers I was mad at. They were just guys trying to feed families and pay for their rigs. I learned on good authority that Baker encouraged drivers to borrow money from his bank to buy new trucks, then repossessed the vehicles if the guys couldn't make their payments. Not one truck came up the road the next day. Nor the next. I slept in blissful peace until 7:00 a.m. But the mining went on. We could hear the rock breaker all day. My neighbors and I wondered what Baker was up to.

After a quiet weekend the noise of trucks again assaulted us going up the hill before dawn. Some came back down from the mine with Jake brakes blaring the whole way as if to say, "Nobody stops Baker!" George Breaker, I thought. He certainly broke the whole neighborhood's sleep. Some days I felt like he was slowly breaking me.

We found out why the trucks were back after about six phone calls. Baker had asked his friend Pete Rahn, the top guy in NMDOT, to obtain a variance from Governor Johnson that would allow him to haul heavier than legal loads on the road for the duration of his contract with BOR, however long that was. I got a copy of the variance and read it. I noted that Rahn presented the request to the governor as though the Bureau of Reclamation needed the riprap because of an emergency even though they were just stockpiling the rock for future needs.

The feat was a breathtaking display of Baker's power and ability to manipulate government at any level, including the governor's office. Baker had obtained the variance in three business days. I felt angry and defeated and impressed.

Along with the information about the variance we learned that SR 582 might be "improved" at taxpayer expense. Translation: NMDOT would upgrade the road for Baker's benefit. Then we would be terrorized by eighteen-wheelers forever.

I had a conversation with a woman in Senator Pete Domenici's office who talked to several people at BOR about regulations governing Baker's mining. At first she got different stories, but after a few calls Garry Rowe, the head honcho at the Albuquerque office, issued a stance everyone fell in line with. He said BOR had no authority to make demands on Baker or inspect his mine site. Rowe was obviously stonewalling.

The destruction at Baker's mine site enraged and sickened me every time I visited. Why was he not mining in another area where there were no petroglyphs? I knew the answer. Baker always did what was cheap and easy.

At the May meeting of Vecinos del Rio we resolved to contact Governor Johnson and ask friends and neighbors to do the same. Our issue was safety. The community would be in peril as long as eighteen-wheelers sped along the road. The governor needed to understand that ours is a small, traditional farming community where many families still have a couple of cows, grow chiles, corn, and alfalfa, and have kitchen gardens. They use and tend the ancient acequias that run through northern New Mexico like arteries branching from the Rio Grande. Some local families have toiled and prospered on the fertile soil created by the river for ten or fifteen generations. Many still gather wood from the forests for heating their homes. Place gives their lives meaning. On any given day there would be farm equipment, kids on bikes, pedestrians, passenger cars, school buses, dogs, occasional livestock, and horses on the road.

Katherine Wells

The situation reflects northern New Mexico's cultural dilemma. People who long subsisted comfortably in an agricultural economy can no longer do so. They no longer own or have free access to traditionally communal lands where they once hunted and fished for food. They cannot barter corn or chiles for farm equipment or fertilizer. They have no option but to become part of the cash economy. That has left them vulnerable to people like Baker. His wealth increases thanks to people who have few alternatives other than driving trucks for low wages. Baker's extractive practices contribute to the destruction of the culture as well as the land. Mining provides short-term jobs and cash, but builds nothing for the future. When Baker is through mining natural resources he will leave with a pocket full of money. The jobs will be gone and the land ruined.

Northern New Mexico is traditionally Democratic, but many in the area had voted for Johnson, a Republican. If Johnson wanted to maintain that support he needed to listen. I thought perhaps we could appeal to him as a bicyclist. He was well known for his passion for the sport. I doubted he would have wanted to ride our road. Baker's eighteen-wheelers would suck the hair right off his legs.

By the latter part of May Vecinos del Rio, my neighbors, and I were battling Baker on several fronts. We had circulated petitions and collected hundreds of signatures that we presented to NMDOT. We had made a presentation before our county commissioners, were working with both of our senators, and trying to get a meeting with Governor Johnson, who had received a blizzard of letters and postcards from us.

My neighbor Mary and I thought our best bet might be to seek help from the attorney general. We were fed up and ready to try anything. Before Baker's variance we were on the verge of barring the road and forcing the state police to issue citations to overweight trucks. I didn't care if I got arrested. We were beginning to get some publicity in the newspapers and that would churn up more press coverage.

One benefit from the struggle with Baker was that I got to know more of my neighbors, like peppery Mrs. Alire who lived on social security. She never missed a Vecinos meeting and donated what she could from her limited income. She didn't care how much money and power Baker had. Wrong was wrong. She would speak out anywhere, anytime.

I also became good friends with Elias and Lupita, who are apple growers. He is a retired college administrator and she worked as an administrator for the state. Both were born in the area and had followed Baker's schemes for decades.

On the night of May 21st we got a hefty rain, but still the trucks arrived at 5:00 a.m. About 6:00 a.m. a truck going uphill got stuck on a patch of concrete embedded in the dirt road just below the house where the grade is very steep. The noise woke the whole neighborhood as the driver tried over and over to get up the road. While he was straining a loaded truck came down the hill. That driver had to back up almost a mile to the mine and get a tractor to come down to pull the stuck truck out and up. Baker quickly sent out a couple of dump trucks full of sand to put over the spot so it would be easier for the trucks to get up the road.

In spite of the sand, another truck got stuck at about 10:30 a.m. I was walking up to the new house site with the dogs and heard the rig struggling. Suddenly there was a booming noise. Then silence. Oh boy, I thought and turned to run down the hill. The truck had jackknifed and gone over the side. The hill below sloped at about a forty-five-degree angle. By the time I got there the driver had emerged from the cab and was climbing up the slope. "Are you okay?" I yelled. He nodded that he was. When he was safely back on the road he said that he wasn't in the truck when it went over. I asked him what he meant. He just repeated the refrain. I couldn't imagine what motivated him to say that unless he thought the statement would mollify Baker. The truck, upside down on the hillside, appeared to be finished.

Everyone on the house crew had come running to see what happened. I commented that I was glad the truck had fallen into an area where there weren't any petroglyphs. The driver of the destroyed truck snarled to another trucker who had arrived that I thought my "damned petroglyphs were more important than his truck." He was right. I did.

My neighbor Leon called the *Rio Grande Sun* and the *Santa Fe New Mexican*. Both sent reporters. The state police came, as did Baker's compliance officer Earl Garcia. Later, two oversized tow trucks arrived with big cranes attached. They started work about 1:00 p.m., saying it would take an hour or so to pull the truck up. A small crowd from the neighborhood gathered to watch the proceedings. The drivers of a couple of

The wreckage of one of Baker's trucks that jack-knifed and went over the side of the hill on our road. Photo by the author.

Baker's trucks already at the mine at the time of the accident were unable to get their loads down so they parked and joined the group. A while later Baker's machinery operators showed up. The house crew went back to work for an hour or so.

Everyone wanted to leave by 3:30. It was Friday and all the guys needed to get to the bank and cash checks before kicking back for the weekend. Three-thirty came and went; then 4:00 p.m., 5:00 p.m., and 6:00 p.m. The retrieval operation ceased to be entertaining. Tempers frayed. The house crew was hot, tired, and ready for a beer. Lloyd lost his temper. For a minute I thought he was going to square off with Earl Garcia. I was ready to punch Garcia myself. He kept insisting in an obnoxious and arrogant manner that Baker owned the whole road, including the half mile through our land. He repeated over and over that he had proof on the survey at his office. His attitude was galling. I was sure that being Baker's shill required that kind of bluff, but his assertion struck me as stupid.

I was in a state because the tow truck with the biggest crane was parked exactly six feet from the petroglyph of the figure with the sun head that was so dear to me. As the machine strained and the crane arm jerked back and forth I worried that something would snap or a big jolt would send machinery crashing into the glyph. I stood as close to the glyph as I could, hearing Baker's guys mutter rude remarks.

At 7:00 p.m. the crane operators finally pulled the truck's trailer over the edge of the road. They wanted to continue working until they could lift the cab, but Lloyd wouldn't let them. He insisted they get the truck trailer out of the way and their machinery off the road so that our crew and Baker's guys could go home. The operators grumbled but did what he said. A cheer went up from all the workers, ours and Baker's. Lloyd was my shining hero at that moment.

The crane operators resumed their work but didn't pull the truck cab up until long after dark.

In addition to Earl Garcia insisting we didn't own the road and the trucker claiming he wasn't in the truck when it went over the side there was another peculiar footnote to the accident. The next day I talked to the reporter who wrote a small article for the *Santa Fe New Mexican*. I wanted to thank him for his reporting. He had called Baker a few hours after the accident to get a quote from him. Baker told him, "That happened yesterday." I couldn't fathom why Baker would tell such a fatuous lie to a reporter who had been on the scene. Perhaps it was his way of saying, "Screw you." It wasn't the first time he had told a whopper.

Nine

The year 1997 was the worst of my life in some ways, but as an exhibiting artist that year was the best. In the spring I had a one-person show titled "Bent Political" at the Center for Contemporary Arts (CCA) in Santa Fe. Most of my work by that time included social commentary. My first requirement was that every piece be aesthetically appealing and well crafted. Beyond that I gave vent to my angst about the state of the world, but I strove to give each piece a sense of presence and to avoid being didactic.

For the CCA show I included some of my nontraditional Guadalupe images and pieces that address children and violence in our culture. One was a small work in a green-painted frame shaped somewhat like a schoolhouse. Inside the frame were seven three-inch-long .270-caliber bullets that I wrapped with the colorful paper labels from Crayola crayons. Above the schoolhouse an American flag waved in red, white, and blue. The backside of the flag was a dollar bill. The unspeakable tragedy of Columbine, Colorado, occurred a couple years later.

In August I had my first museum show, a milestone for any artist, at the Sun Cities Museum of Art in Arizona. The director gave me a large space and I decided to treat the show somewhat like a retrospective of my mixed-media sculpture. I titled the exhibit "Slouching Toward the Millennium," misquoting and alluding to W. B. Yeats's poem "The Second Coming." Like Yeats I believe that our culture is sleepwalking into a catastrophic future.

I had to rent a small U-Haul truck to get the work to Arizona. My dry-eye problem made it impossible for me to drive to the Phoenix area myself. A friend went along to drive. After we unloaded the work and returned the truck she flew back to Albuquerque. I stayed for the show opening that took place a couple of days later.

In addition to nontraditional Guadalupe figures I showed several large cross images that were nontraditional in nature as well as some new work using circuit boards and pieces from several series I had done in the late 1980s.

The invitation for the exhibit featured one of my crosses. The sculpture was a deep blue cross-shaped wooden box about thirty inches high that I had made and painted. Inside it I placed rows of shiny high-caliber rifle bullets wrapped in tiny American flags. I arranged the bullets in chevron-shaped rows and titled the piece *God Bless America*. It dazzled.

An article appeared in the local paper about the show and my iconoclastic images. Someone apparently sent a copy of the article to a man back East who was the head of a Catholic lay organization. The museum director received a letter from the gentleman lambasting the museum and everyone associated with it for exhibiting such vile and blasphemous work. The man had not seen the show; he had just read an article about the exhibit featuring one photograph in black and white. The director received another letter from a group of nuns who had come to the exhibit. They wrote a letter saying they were moved to tears by my work and encouraged the museum to show more work with such depth and candor. I thought of framing the two letters and hanging them side-by-side in my studio.

I was also part of a four-person show at Guadalupe Fine Art in Santa Fe with the cross as its theme. In spite of the unconventional nature of my crosses, most of them sold. For one of them I constructed a three-foot-high, black, cross-shaped box about four inches deep. From yard sales and thrift stores I gathered dozens of pairs of tiny, worn children's shoes. I painted them all black and glued them into the cross overlapping and crowding each other. I placed small toys, tiny doll parts, and

God Bless America, mixed-media sculpture with bullets wrapped with tiny American flags, 40" x 28" x 1½". In private collection. Photo by Pat Pollard.

bullets into some of the shoes. After dyeing all the shoestrings black I knotted them and tied them diagonally back and forth across the piece. I gave the work depth by painting the edges of some of the shoes, toys, and strings with iridescent blue and orange paint. I titled the piece *Blessed Are the Children*. The work is dark but so is reality for millions of children in our world.

A review of the exhibit in the *Santa Fe New Mexican* said my work was not for the "faint of heart." The week after the opening the gallery owner called to tell me that the priest from the church in San Juan Pueblo had read the article and come to see the exhibit. He sat with the *Blessed Are the Children* piece for half an hour. He said the work was the only fresh expression of the essence of Christianity that he had seen in decades. I had never met the priest and he had never heard of me. He wanted the work for the church in San Juan but had no budget for art. He had a wealthy parishioner he hoped could be persuaded to buy the piece. The plan failed, but I gave the cross to the church on a long-term loan. I never, ever imagined having my art in a Catholic church: Unitarian maybe, but not Catholic.

In retrospect I have no idea how I managed to hang three shows in the chaos of fighting Baker, building a house, getting dinner on the table every night, and dealing with a man physically and psychologically wrestling with cancer. I had committed to two of the shows more than a year before and created most of the art for them in 1996. I didn't exhibit at all in 1998 because I lacked both the time and energy to create anything in 1997 except a house and a big stink.

A newspaper article had been published about George Baker's mining operation a couple of weeks before the truck-over-the-side-of-the-road episode. The story had a serendipitous result. A man named Harry Wilson, who was a retired Bureau of Reclamation engineer, looked up the phone number of my neighbor Mary, who was quoted in the piece. Mary lived about a mile south of us on the mesa and could hear Baker's mining machinery and trucks almost as well as we could. She had spent countless hours working with me and others on the problem. Mary called to tell me about Harry, saying that he wanted to meet with us and help out however he could. Harry lived in Los Alamos but had been the engineer on a local diversion dam project that BOR had done several years back. He had spent considerable time in the area and visited some of the petroglyphs.

Harry had contacted the Albuquerque office of the Bureau of Reclamation and obtained a copy of their contract with Baker. He told Mary that BOR was violating several regulations. Mary and I met with Harry, who was very formal in his manner. He was disturbed by BOR's actions and appeared genuine in his desire to help.

Harry was in his sixties and could not have been retired from BOR for more than a few years. From his thirty-year career with the agency he knew BOR upside down and backward. Here was a priceless ally. Things were looking up.

Harry showed us BOR's contract with Baker that he had obtained. It stated that Baker would supply them with thirty-four thousand tons of riprap. We did some rough calculations and determined that he had already hauled out at least half the material. Given the number of trucks running each day he should finish by the end of the summer. That information was a huge relief to me because of the house and continual sleep deprivation. But that would not be the end of it. I wanted to prevent Baker from mining on the mesa in the future if possible, or failing that, to know for damn sure that any further mining and the hauling on SR 582 would be done according to the law governing the mining and hauling on the road.

One of Baker's contract violations was that the document specified only stockpiled material was to be provided. Another violation was that an archaeological survey was supposed to be completed, but it had not been done. BOR claimed that a survey was not required on private land in spite of the fact their regulations stated otherwise. Harry thought that Baker and the Bureau of Reclamation were not keeping proper records or following required safety procedures. Nor was Baker tarping his trucks or providing dust abatement with water trucks as the contract specified. Harry ticked off item after item that BOR and Baker were ignoring. He couldn't be buffaloed by them. Hallelujah, I mumbled under my breath.

After meeting with us Harry began writing an endless string of letters that I typed. They were often several pages long. He addressed them to various people at BOR, Senators Domenici and Bingaman, Congressman Redman, Lynne Sebastian, the state historic preservation officer, Attorney General Udall, the Corps of Engineers, the Environmental Protection Agency, and several other governmental offices. With most letters I sent copies to at least six different people.

I loathe typing. My mother made me take two years of typing in high school because she wanted me to be a secretary. I took one year of shorthand for the same reason. I showed no aptitude for shorthand and not much more for typing. Being a secretary was at the bottom of my preferred occupations list. The battle with Baker and the Bureau of Reclamation is one of the reasons I'm glad my mother was insistent.

I had only surrendered to the world of computers a few months before. On my son Tas's advice I bought a Mac and a printer. He thought Macs were more user friendly than PCs and thus more suitable for the technologically challenged like me. He, of course, would never condescend to use anything but a PC. I hated giving up my IBM Selectric, which I loved passionately for its error correction feature. Before the advent of the Selectric I spent half my time using one of those round, skinny typewriter erasers with a brush attached.

I took the plunge into the computer age in part so I would have some inkling of what computers are about. Tas and a friend owned a growing software company by then and I felt I had do something to transcend the world of dinosaurs. When I found myself typing scores of letters and sending out multiple copies I realized I could not have done that without a computer and printer. My skills were primitive but they sufficed.

One of the first letters Harry wrote was to Garry Rowe, the guy in charge of the Bureau of Reclamation in Albuquerque requesting copies of eighteen Reclamation documents pertaining to their contract with Baker under the Freedom of Information Act. The letter went out, as all of them did, over the name of the Vecinos del Rio secretary. Rowe's underlings supplied a few of the items, but others never materialized. Harry thought that some of them didn't even exist although Reclamation's regs required them.

As May wore on I paid precious little attention to house construction. Freddie had come to work again and Pablo asked for his job back. I wanted to have him on the crew but felt I didn't have the energy or time to deal with him. I told Pablo to come talk to me again in a couple of weeks.

I had scant time to do art or enjoy hiking and the petroglyphs. No more hours of exploring, visiting, and revisiting favorite images. I hiked to Baker's mine on Sundays when the machines were blessedly idle and the road quiet. The great Awanyu remained in place with its companion glyphs, but one image of a human figure on a rock near the road was gone. Over and over I walked around the area where the boulder had been. Had the rock ended up on a truck? Did a bulldozer move it or turn it over? I never found out. Fortunately I had a photo of the figure that I had taken before Baker bought the land. My pals from Vecinos del Rio and I joked—or half joked—about having the image put on milk cartons. Have you seen this petroglyph?

Fighting Baker had become a full-time job, an obsession. With the entry of Harry into the fray my workload accelerated. Harry mailed or personally delivered many letters every week. He wrote each one in neat block print on a legal-sized yellow pad, which I then typed. Harry had become the general in our campaign and I his chief aide.

I typed my inept fingers to the bone. We assumed that BOR understood that Harry was the real author of the letters. Harry's writing was stiff and full of government-speak; it revealed knowledge of the agency that no one would have believed the secretary of Vecinos del Rio or me or anyone who didn't work for BOR would possess.

My neck hurt from so much time on the phone, and my back ached from too many hours at the computer. The surface of my eyes felt like the Mojave Desert. Sometimes Lloyd tried to get me to slack off, but I would not. I could not.

After many requests the Albuquerque office of the Bureau of Reclamation granted us a meeting with the brass on June 6th. Mary and I and oth-ers from Vecinos figured we would have to drive down to Albuquerque to their office. Harry said no, no, no. Make them come here. And they did.

Garry Rowe, Bill Rowher, and two others came. I enjoyed being able to put faces to the names of the disembodied voices I had been talking to on the phone and writing to for months. They all filed into my living room carrying brown or gray briefcases. I served iced tea and store-bought cookies. Mary, Rose, Harry, a couple of my neighbors, and I represented Vecinos. Everyone looked uncomfortable except Harry. The people from BOR smiled pleasant, conservative smiles and appeared to have been cut from the same bureaucratic cloth. Garry Rowe looked like he had spent his entire life in an office.

My neighbor Gilbert Romero attended the meeting. What he lacked in articulateness Gilbert made up for in loudness. The meeting had barely started when he stood up and launched into a fifteen-minute tirade about what a crook Baker was and what a bunch of *cabrones malcriados* worked for BOR. He threw in his grievances about some work BOR had done on the local acequia a few years back. It had totally screwed up the job and now the ditch silted in every year. Why the hell didn't they fix it? he asked. I enjoyed watching the pained expressions on the faces of the captive bureaucrats.

Garry Rowe politely reiterated what he had said on the phone and in letters: that he and BOR had no jurisdiction over Baker's actions. "Has the agency changed its regs since I retired?" Harry asked calmly. Rowe admitted they had not. "Then you do have jurisdiction," Harry responded. Rowe insisted the way the regulations were being interpreted had changed. He agreed to contact those who had jurisdiction and report back to us.

The whole performance was an exercise in blowing smoke. "Time to go up the chain of command," Harry said afterward with exasperation. He had already begun having me copy Charles Calhoun, the regional director of the Bureau of Reclamation in Salt Lake City, on all his letters.

The day after the meeting my neighbor Sally called to tell me that a co-worker of hers who lives north of us had seen one of Baker's trucks pass a school bus that had stopped to let kids off about a mile north on the road that afternoon. I wanted to talk to the woman and see if she would make a statement. Sally said no. The woman said she wanted us to know about the incident, but she was unwilling to get involved. Someone in her family probably worked for Baker.

That afternoon foreshadowed an incident that took place a couple of years later. A child was struck and killed by a truck belonging to one of Baker's many companies. It made me want to shoot him. Baker denied any connection with the vehicle. What kind of human being allows his employees to speed and drive around school buses?

There were times I tried to see Baker's side of the story: that of a businessman trying to make money. I had no objection to making money, but doing so at the expense of your own community was beyond the pale. I wondered if he ever looked at the larger picture or imagined

The choking, ever-present dust from one of Baker's
untarped rock trucks. Photo by the author.

what a positive force he could be in the area if he used his money to pro-
mote education or fight the drug problem.

A few days after the meeting Vecinos members had a meeting with
Attorney General Tom Udall. Twenty people from the neighborhood
and Vecinos drove to his office in Santa Fe. We presented our grievances
against the Bureau of Reclamation and NMDOT. Udall listened atten-
tively. Assistant District Attorney Letty Belin took notes furiously. Udall
agreed to write a letter to Pete Rahn, investigate the constitutionality
of the variance, and go to school on BOR's regulations and whether or
not they were being enforced. We left with the feeling that we had been
heard and that Udall would follow up as he said he would.

In mid-May Lloyd and I made calls to Earl Garcia and to BOR
requesting water trucks on our road to dampen the dirt. The dust had
become horrific. Great clouds of the stuff choked us every day. We could

hear trucks moving up and down the road, but could barely see them for the billowing dust. The Bureau of Reclamation insisted they had no authority to make Baker use water trucks. Earl promised he would send one but never did.

For weeks Mary and I tried to schedule a meeting with Governor Johnson with no success. We sent Johnson copies of petitions with hundreds of signatures of people opposing the use of the road by eighteen-wheelers. We wracked our brains about what we could do to make him understand how vital a safe road is to local people.

Finally, Johnson's scheduler called and said he would grant us a fifteen-minute meeting. Rose and I and three other Vecinos members drove to Santa Fe. A secretary ushered us into a room with a round table and dark blue carpeting. Johnson came in after a few minutes flanked by his aides. Good grief, I thought, he's like royalty.

I told Johnson I had ridden a bicycle across Tierra del Fuego, the length of Arizona, and half the length of California, but was afraid to ride through my neighborhood. He looked nonplussed. I didn't want the meeting to be pro forma. We presented our complaints. Johnson said he had been led to believe that Baker was hauling rock for BOR on an emergency basis. He made no promises but said he would see what he could do. Knowing his bias toward business no one in our group expected much.

By the middle of June the number of trucks coming up the hill every day began to decrease and Baker started sending water trucks, probably because he was being pressured by BOR. One drove up and down the road several times a day—even when it was raining.

Our construction crew had finished the bond beam on the house and had begun putting up decking. The ceiling in the house would be rough-sawed pine boards except in the living room area, which had clerestory windows. There we used split *latillas* that are traditional in New Mexico. A lot of rain fell in mid-June and slowed everything down. Lloyd and I hoped the roof would be on before the beginning of the monsoon rains.

In late June Lloyd received a message from his doctor giving him the results of his latest PSA test. The number was 4.0. The first post-radiation test he had taken in March yielded a reassuringly low score. This one was disconcerting. Four was the top of the normal range, but the speed with which the number had risen was worrisome. Lloyd felt fine, but I knew the news was chewing his insides.

Lloyd had begun to grumble about Ernie. With trucks on the road and the Baker battle on my mind I didn't pay much attention. He said Ernie didn't have any sense of aesthetics. Once or twice he called him a block-headed Dutchman. Lloyd and Ernie got in an argument one afternoon about the shape of the parapets. The crew had hauled pumicecrete up to the roof and poured it into the wooden parapet forms Lloyd had built. After the forms were removed, Ernie began applying a scratch coat of stucco to the parapets. He rounded the tops so that water would run off and not create a leak hazard. Lloyd insisted they should be flat on top. Ernie insisted they should be rounded. Lloyd backed off, but he seethed.

I went inside the house to the area that would be our bedroom to think about closet design. When I walked back toward the entry I heard Lloyd and Ernie yelling at each other. They were standing between the table saw and Ernie's truck. Their bodies were tensed and ready for action. Their faces red and ugly. "You don't have any more brains than a goddamned brick," Lloyd snarled.

"And you don't know what the hell you're talking about," Ernie retorted.

"It's my house and the parapets are going to be flat."

"We're either gonna to do it the right way or I'm outta here," Ernie parried.

"Good enough for me." Lloyd turned and walked slowly down the driveway toward the small house. I stood in horror with my heart pounding as though it might break through my ribs. Good God, what was I supposed to do now? The whole crew stood staring with vacant faces. Ernie squeezed a tape measure he held in his hand and watched Lloyd's retreating figure. A sudden, silent tableau.

Ernie and I had become friends and I thought he was doing a

creditable job. I agreed with his logic about the parapets. He didn't have Lloyd's refined sensibility about architecture, but he knew how to follow plans and build a solid house. I had no regrets about hiring him.

I walked over to the studio and hung onto the door frame. For a few minutes I thought I might faint. I have low blood pressure and since my late thirties have often passed out under emotional and physical duress. The stress had been awful every day for months, but what I had just witnessed was a bomb. I wished I could suddenly be teleported to Alpha Centauri or any place else.

I couldn't hide out in the studio all day. Should I tell Lloyd he was behaving like a jackass? Should I remind him that it was really my house, not his? Remind him that I was paying him as part of the crew? Tell him that if he couldn't behave I didn't want him on it? And what should I tell Ernie? The house was only half finished. I needed his help and he was counting on the job. The dilemma sat in my stomach like lead. Ernie and I talked for a moment. I told him I had no idea what would happen. "Do what you have to do," he said.

I walked down the road feeling like my whole life was coming apart. Hell, it *was* coming apart. I had no clue what I would say to Lloyd. I wanted to get in my car and drive until I had put at least a thousand miles between this place and me. A truck had just gone down the road. Dust hung in the air like a brown shroud.

I walked in the house and saw Lloyd slumped on the couch, his battered tool belt on the floor beside him. The red suspenders he always wore to keep his jeans up when he donned a tool belt provided a discordant colorful note in the pall that filled the room. I sat down on one of the dining chairs facing Lloyd. Its stained seat cover needed reupholstering. I made a mental note to do that before we moved into the new house. If we moved in.

Lloyd and I sat in prickly silence for ten or fifteen minutes. I decided to let him break it. He had sawdust in his hair and looked older than I had ever seen him look. Neither of us tried to make eye contact.

"I guess I'll be moving out," he said, looking at his work-scarred hands. His voice was softer than normal. Angry as I was, Lloyd's words made my throat tighten. I didn't think he would have said that if he didn't mean it.

Katherine Wells

"You really think that's the answer?" I replied, rubbing my eyes. The question sat there like a dead weight. I thought about Lloyd's health and what the future held. Neither of us spoke, but he finally looked up. "You need me," I said. After a slight pause my voice continued of its own accord, "And I need you." Lloyd digested that for a couple of minutes, then stood up and walked toward the back door, pausing to touch me on the shoulder. He said he was going for a drive so he could think. He went out to his truck and left.

I walked up the hill to face Ernie.

The crew was cleaning up for the day. Ernie and I went into the studio and sat down. He understood what a predicament I was in. "It's okay," he said. "Not the end of the world." He apologized for his own outburst. I told him I didn't know how the dilemma would play out but that I felt I had to stick with Lloyd even though he was wrongheaded about the parapets and had acted like a jackass. I assured Ernie I didn't think he had done anything to deserve such ire.

"It's about Lloyd, not about you," I said. We both felt Lloyd was building a monument to himself and as such could not stand to have the work done any way but his. I thought more about it that night as I tried to sleep and wondered why I had not seen what was going on before. The house was Lloyd's last hurrah. His PSA test results must have frightened him even though he wouldn't discuss the subject. I should have known from the beginning that since he designed the house he would not be able to give up control.

The next morning Lloyd went up the hill prepared to work. Ernie was already there. Lloyd apologized for his behavior and started sanding the entry door he was building. By some process I did not understand he and Ernie came to an accord. Ernie began packing up his tools and equipment. He was gone by noon. Two of the guys he had brought to the job went with him. Jack stayed. As difficult as Jack was, he and Lloyd appreciated each other's craftsmanship.

The number of trucks on the road began to decrease in inverse proportion to the number of letters issuing from Harry's blue ballpoint pen. In July and August he wrote multiple letters to Garry Rowe, State

Historic Preservation Officer Lynne Sebastian, Senator Pete Domenici, Attorney General Tom Udall, and Reclamation Commissioner Eluid Martinez in Washington who, as it happened, was from a nearby town. He also addressed the Environmental Protection Agency, the New Mexico Mining and Minerals Division, Regional Bureau of Reclamation Director Charles Calhoun, and the environmental officer of San Juan Pueblo. We received copies of the letters each official wrote to Rowe and Rowe's replies and replies to replies. A forest of paper was on the move.

The point we hammered on most with BOR was the fact that the agency had not required Baker to conduct an archaeological survey of his mining sites. BOR swore a survey was not required on private land. Harry knew they were wrong. The Bureau of Reclamation also said repeatedly that Baker had done an archaeological survey of his mine sites, but never produced a copy. I thought Baker was referring to the recording that three of my friends from the Archaeological Society of New Mexico's Rock Art Field School had done in 1995.

Baker had switched locations without telling BOR. He mined rather than providing them stockpiled materials as the contract specified. We told BOR, but they did not believe us. The agency continued with the myth that a survey was not required. Reclamation stonewalled us on the local, regional, and national level. By July we knew we were causing them serious pain. We felt sure their employees were spending untold hours trying to cover up the fact that the agency had turned a blind eye to the way Baker did things.

When Baker first bought the land he drove up the dirt road frequently to check on some bulldozer project he had going. He said he was looking for water, which seemed unlikely. His bulldozer operator made a hole more than twenty feet deep. Lloyd and I drove up the road behind him one day and introduced ourselves. We wanted to know if Baker would sell us a twenty-acre parcel adjacent to our property that had a lot of petroglyphs. Baker told us to send him a letter pointing out where the parcel was and he would think about the idea. He never responded to our letter.

While we were there I thought I might as well ask Baker if my Rock

Katherine Wells

Art Field School friends and I could record the area of the big Awanyu and the large upside-down figure. Baker was focused on the bulldozer's maneuvers and only half listening. "Yeah, I guess it's all right if it's for a school," he said absently. I took that as a yes. I told him he would receive copies of all the information we collected. Three of my friends and I recorded those glyph areas a few weeks later. Unfortunately we recorded only the side of the meadow with the Awanyu and attendant glyphs; no one took a careful look at the areas he was now mining.

I had sent copies of our recording work to Baker and the originals went to ARMS. Of course BOR couldn't produce Baker's copy as proof that there had been a survey. That would have proved what we contended—that Reclamation had not followed the law because they had not required him to do a survey of the area he was actually mining.

By the 11th of July the truck traffic had almost stopped. Baker had delivered the thirty-four thousand tons of rock his contract called for. Funnily enough, in response to pressure from the attorney general, NMDOT rescinded Baker's variance on the 8th of July. Such timing. Baker no doubt received the letter on the eleventh.

Though trucks no longer awakened us before dawn and no longer terrorized us on the dirt road or SR 582, my workload decreased little. The fight with the Bureau of Reclamation would go on and so would the struggle with NMDOT about keeping the fourteen-ton load limit on the road.

I also had to devote a lot more attention to the house project. When Ernie and his guys pulled off the job and Lloyd took over, I had to take on the job of general contractor again. I had called Pablo to come back on the crew a couple of weeks before the big blowup. He had brought a guy who turned out to be both good and bad news. Nick was a skilled and talented plasterer and charming, but he was also a drug addict and you couldn't believe anything he said. Both habits made him unreliable. I hated giving him his paycheck because I knew where the money would go. He had a beautiful nine-year-old daughter he brought by to see the house one Saturday. Nick said he seldom saw her. I didn't know whether that was good or bad for the girl given his habit. One of Jack's brothers joined the crew as well. We had enough help, but now I had to keep the crews' hours and generally tend to them. And I was again in charge of procuring materials, but not happily so.

The roof was finished by the end of July. The monsoon could do its worst and work would continue inside the house unimpeded. To celebrate, Lloyd and I went to the Spanish Market, which is always held the fourth weekend of July on the plaza in Santa Fe. Traditional Spanish Colonial arts had been experiencing a revival in recent years. Images of saints painted as retablos or carved as three-dimensional bultos, straw-inlay work, tinwork, and other arts and crafts in Spanish Colonial style are displayed and sold for their artistic and cultural value. Lloyd and I bought an exquisite punched-tin light fixture for the house.

In August Lloyd and I shut the job down for a couple of days and took a long weekend trip to Telluride, Colorado. I desperately needed to get away for a bit and I always enjoy going to high mountain areas. I love the cool air, the smell of sun on pine needles, and mountain wildflowers. Telluride is upscale touristy, which means lots of good restaurants. Lloyd wanted to go there because the place is a Mecca for hang gliding. He wanted to learn how to hang glide. I didn't think the sport was the best thing to pursue at his present stage of life, but it was his life. We took a shuttle up to the high mountain perch from which hang gliders launched. Lloyd and I watched many of the brightly colored conveyances take to the air and float on thermals with the ease of hawks.

Between Lloyd's preoccupation with sailing and his lust to be airborne I wondered that he stayed home at all. In addition to the tether that I provided, I thought perhaps his need to create with his hands was the chief thing that kept him on land.

Ten

On July 25, 1997, Harry and I and a few others from Vecinos del Rio had a meeting at Baker's upper mine site with members of Garry Rowe's staff to discuss several issues: the possibility of removing George Baker from the Bureau of Reclamation's bidders list, changes in Reclamation policy that would help prevent the kind of problems that had arisen with Baker's contract, potentially serious erosion problems caused by the mining, Baker's alleged archaeological survey, and other points. At last BOR was listening. Harry was determined to continue the struggle until they took full responsibility for their actions.

We all stood in the late morning heat viewing the devastation wrought by Baker's machines on one side of the ruined meadow and the giant Awanyu figure and other glyphs on the other. One of the glyphs depicts a charming copulation scene. Male and female stand side by side. The male has an extraordinary penis, which makes a right turn below his feet and travels over to the female where it turns upward toward her vagina. A daunting performance. The figures represent fertility, no doubt. Now they occupied a sterile and ravaged landscape.

A couple of curious matters regarding the Bureau of Reclamation arose later that summer of 1997. Harry had obtained an internal memo written by an unidentified author, an archaeologist, stating that "it IS" the agency's responsibility to protect archaeological resources on private land when working with a contractor, just as Harry insisted. Harry was on a mission to discover who had written the memo.

A few weeks later Reclamation archaeologist Rob Freed signed and had notarized a statement that I typed. He verified that the author of the memo was Dr. Signa Larralde, an archaeologist who worked in the regional office in Salt Lake City. Rob Freed had by then transferred from Albuquerque to a Reclamation office in another region. Harry said his move reflected Freed's unhappiness at the way things were being done in Albuquerque. The agency soon transferred Dr. Larralde to the agency's Albuquerque office.

As part of the continuing campaign after Baker had fulfilled his contract, Harry wrote Freedom of Information Act requests to BOR over and over but we never received more than a few documents. We thought letters we received from the regional office in Salt Lake and Reclamation headquarters in Washington were condescending and evasive. Harry just kept the queries flowing, knowing that they had to respond and that the letters would have an erosive effect. During the rest of the summer and fall, though, the paper war was at its height.

At one point a copy of an e-mail sent by Garry Rowe's secretary to someone else in the agency came into our hands. The communication didn't contain much useful information, but the woman said "let's get this monkey off our back," referring to Vecinos del Rio. In a way I didn't blame her. We caused her and others a lot of work. I suspect her boss had made us seem like arch villains.

By the first of September all the windows were in place in the house and Lloyd, assisted by Nick and Freddie, who worked the cement mixer, had put a scratch coat of stucco on the outside of the entire building.

I felt reassured standing at a distance and looking at the house with a coat of stucco. At times the whole project seemed so big and chaotic and slow that I just wanted to run away. The house construction was (again) a major stressor, even without the Baker struggle. The new house was more than twice the size of the small one and four times as complicated.

Katherine Wells

Lloyd's perfectionism nearly drove me to commit mayhem. I wanted to scream, "Just get it done!" when he fussed over tiny details.

Our neighbor Cindy's parents were visiting from back east. They had never heard of a straw-bale house, let alone seen one. Cindy called to ask if they could stop by and have a look. They came on a particularly hot afternoon in the middle of a crisis. The electrician had gone AWOL. He had said he would be there two days earlier, then yesterday, then today. His absence held up work a couple of the other guys were waiting to do. Lloyd acted as though I was supposed to pull another electrician out of my hat.

Cindy came in with her parents, who were wide-eyed. I showed them around a bit. "Why, you're building your dream house," the mother said with innocent wonder in her voice. I managed a tepid smile. I wanted to yell, "No, it's my nightmare house," and unload on her all the miseries of an owner/builder.

The thing that helped me survive the building of the "dream house" was that I had a comfy little dwelling to retreat to. I wasn't frantic to move in as I had been when we lived in the Silver Streak. Lloyd and I hoped to be in the new house by Christmas, but if we weren't I would not care much.

I still found solace in the petroglyphs when I had time to visit them. A special shield bearer sporting jaunty feathers on his head was located about a twenty-minute hike from the house and drew me like a magnet. The fellow has a cheerful-looking face. Turkey tracks surround him and give the panel an animated feeling. The shield bearer stands like a sentinel on the top of a hill. He is a warrior. I am a warrior. We are allies.

Lloyd had his quarterly PSA test in October. The score was 11.8. His doctor said he would probably need to start chemotherapy in a few months. Radiation, we saw clearly, had slowed the cancer's growth for the better part of a year, but not for a few years as we had hoped. We were both devastated that all those magic rays had not produced a more lasting effect.

At home the evening after his doctor's appointment we were both feeling glum. We sat at the table for a bit after dinner. "I hate it," I complained while making swirls in the leftover marinara sauce on my plate with my finger. Lloyd looked at me and quipped, "Don't worry, I've

My "ally," a classic Puebloan shield-bearer image surrounded by turkey tracks.

Katherine Wells

already outlived my brain by five years." Lloyd and I had both reached the age where names, keys, phone numbers, glasses, and many other things deserted or eluded us when we needed them. Lloyd had helped his mother through her last heart-wrenching, gut-wrenching years of Alzheimer's. Cancer, he felt, was a preferable fate to Alzheimer's.

In early November Lloyd went to Mexico to his boat. He would be home before Thanksgiving. While he was gone some of the guys would continue working on the house under my supervision. I certainly wouldn't trust Jack to run any part of my country but I did trust him to install my cupboards.

Harry's letter-writing campaign did not slack off even in December. On the 3rd I typed an epistle to Assistant Attorney General Letty Belin, in which Harry listed nine different agencies we had written to, the dates of all the letters, and whether or not we received a reply. I don't know if Letty was impressed with the number of letters, but I was.

Three days before Christmas I sent a two-page letter detailing the status of our quest with the Bureau of Reclamation to every agency and individual on our lengthy list. I'm not sure Harry had noticed in his single-minded zeal that the holiday approached. I was so grateful for his help that I would have typed letters on Christmas Eve if Harry asked me to.

The new house had doors but no doorknobs on Christmas Day. Only one of the bathrooms had tile. That tiny space off the hall came to be one of my favorite parts of the house. Lloyd had made a beautiful white cement floor in the shower and covered the stall's walls with corrugated sheet metal, a task that turned out to be much more difficult than anticipated. The effect was delightful. For the countertop I crafted faux potsherds with patterns like Pueblo pottery. Every detail of the room came out just right.

With Lloyd's agreement I had hired Ernie to build all the cabinets for the kitchen and bathrooms. As in the small house I wanted to use rough-sawn wood. The cabinets turned out to have warm rosy-gold wood tones. Jack finished installing all the cabinets by the new year, though tile work needed to be finished in the kitchen.

The "dream house" under construction. Photo by the author.

I had engaged a talented solar engineer to design our heating and solar-panel systems. We were able to buy six four-by-eight panels from a company in Albuquerque. We planned to install them on the roof with a wood and metal structure to hold them at the proper angle to the sun. When the crew began to install the thing on the roof Lloyd and I realized immediately that we had made a mistake. The size of the beast made the house look as if it were crowned with a monstrous headdress. We both said no. Lloyd and I scouted around and decided to have the solar panels straddle a small arroyo near the south end of the house.

By the new year the full-time house crew was down to Lloyd and Jack and our friend Chris who had returned from a lengthy visit to New Hampshire. We still had a long list of things to finish up before we moved in, including tile work, getting appliances in and hooked up, sealing all the wood on the windows and window frames, doors and cabinets, final work on the heating system, last minute plumbing and electrical details, building doghouses, and installing lock sets. Lloyd thought we would be able to move in by the middle of February.

Katherine Wells

Completed "dream house" interior, looking toward the kitchen.
Photo by the author.

On February eleventh I looked around in despair at the construction mess. I felt beaten down, but I was too tired to complain. The large worktable that Lloyd and Ernie had built in the living room area was still there. Tools were everywhere. Stray pieces of lumber, buckets, paintbrushes, boxes of nails and screws, pieces of tile, electrical wire, and tarps occupied various rooms and corners.

The next day Chris and Lloyd disassembled the worktable and took it outside. As people carried out tools, tarps, and odds and ends, Chris's girlfriend Teresa and I began cleaning up. About 4:00 in the afternoon I carried a trash container outside. When I walked back in something magical had happened. What had been a giant, painful, energy sucking, money sucking, never ending, horrific project had become a house. And a beautiful house at that. Even better, I was going to live in it.

I stood where the dining table would be, looking at the living room area. Lloyd had designed and built an exquisite, modified shepherd's fireplace with a graceful chimney sweeping to the clerestory ceiling. I turned to the kitchen area we had carefully designed so we could both work there comfortably at the same time. I walked over and stood at the sink. Out the large, east-facing window in front of me was what I thought to be the world's finest view. The perfectly framed mountains lay deep in snow. Afternoon light bathed them in shades of blue.

The mud plaster came alive with the construction mess removed. Lloyd, with Nick as his helper, had created walls that had a warm, pure feeling. The soft earth tones speckled with darker grains of sand and golden flecks of straw were like an elegant meditation in mud. The smoothly rounded corners added to the effect. There were no hard edges.

After the crew went home I sat on the living room floor as winter darkness fell, wondering how anything so beautiful could have emerged from such chaos. Lloyd had nearly driven me crazy with his insistence that every detail be perfect. By the time the house was half built I was ready to cut corners wholesale just to end the torture. Lloyd ignored me and went about every job in his own calm way. And here was the payoff. The place wasn't just a house; it was a work of art. Now I better understood Lloyd's unconscious need to oust Ernie, however badly he had done it. Here stood his opus, his statement of what he could create. I was glad he took his time while I chafed.

We had only been in the house a week. Chris and Teresa had moved into the Silver Streak. The two of them would go back to New Hampshire in the summer, but they much preferred New Mexico winters to the bitter ice and snow of New England. Chris worked with Lloyd finishing the carport and many other jobs that remained to be done outside. Teresa proved to be an enormous help getting the house cleaned up and ready to move into, helping us move, and helping me prepare the small house for rental.

I was in the kitchen talking to houseguests who had arrived from California. The wind thrashed the branches of the junipers outside. Unusual wind for February. I heard a crashing noise at the other end of the house. I couldn't think of anything that could fall and produce such a sound. I walked down the hall and glanced into the room we made into an office, into our bedroom, and then climbed the three stairs to the guest room. Nothing. Then I looked out the south window of the guest room.

Completed "dream house" looking west under peerless
New Mexico skies. Photo by Steven Rudy

There in the arroyo about fifty feet away lay our six solar panels and
pieces of their support structure. Broken glass littered the ground. Lloyd
and Chris stood staring at the disaster, their shirttails whipping in the
wind. The fact that we had houseguests limited the number of expletives
I spouted. I thought about which of the two men outside I was going to
murder first. The two of them had built the framework for the panels,
installed them, and anchored the whole thing to the ground. Lloyd, it
turned out, was the culprit. The framework design called for a row of
bolts on the back of the structure that he had forgotten to put in. The
only good news, more or less, was that only two of the six panels broke.
Lloyd and Chris were able to repair the framework and I had two new
panels delivered from Albuquerque. The second time Lloyd screwed a
double row of bolts through the back timbers.

Eleven

In January 1998 Harry had resumed his duties in our campaign. By then he had written (and I had typed) forty-five long letters to Garry Rowe in Albuquerque and Charles Calhoun in Salt Lake with unsatisfactory results. On the battlefront regarding NMDOT, Harry wrote a letter to Pete Rahn requesting nine different documents under the Freedom of Information Act. We had been pressing to have a public meeting with Rahn and NMDOT since November and to have another meeting with Garry Rowe and his staff at my house.

At the end of January we received a six-page letter from Assistant Attorney General Letty Belin detailing her investigation of our complaints on behalf of Tom Udall. She made it clear that BOR was responsible for environmental impacts on private land as well as public. The letter stated that an agency "should not accept on blind faith" what contractors tell them about mining impacts. My favorite line was "there should have been NHPA (National Historic Preservation Act) consultation before any activity occurred."

I was ready to break out the champagne. Tom Udall and Letty Belin had called BOR to the carpet. Harry reminded me there were still other unresolved issues with the hulking agency.

In February Pete Rahn agreed to a public meeting on March third. We got permission to use the gymnasium at San Juan Pueblo Elementary School. Vecinos del Rio started organizing for the meeting. We all knew this would be our only chance to demonstrate to Pete Rahn how strongly the community felt about maintaining the fourteen-ton load limit on SR 582.

We organized an all-out effort to get the community, friends, and family to show up. I called in all my IOUs from people in Santa Fe I had given petroglyph tours for and contacted others who cared about rock art. Everyone who belonged to Vecinos got on the phone and called everybody they knew in the area. We printed flyers and convinced people who had never been to a public meeting or taken a political stand before that in their own self-interest they had to come to this meeting. We offered rides and made hundreds of last-minute reminder calls.

The meeting was to begin at 7:00 p.m. Several Vecinos members arrived at the school early to set up a sound system and take care of organizational details. I arrived at 6:30. About a dozen eighteen-wheelers lined the sides of the road leading to the school. The school parking lot overflowed. Many people had to park two or three blocks away. I walked into the gym with my heart pounding like I was going to a shoot-out.

At least 250 people crowded the gym and more kept coming in. On the right side of the bleachers sat about fifty truckers. George Baker's white hair and pale features stood out in the center of the mostly Hispano faces. Most of the guys wore baseball caps and plaid flannel shirts. Vecinos members and our supporters filled the rest of the bleachers. People stood two and three deep against the walls. We estimated our total crowd to be at least three hundred—very impressive for a small community composed mainly of people who were loath to participate in anything controversial.

In the afternoon before the meeting Vecinos President Dale Gardner had given Pete Rahn a tour up and down SR 582 so he could see first-hand what the problems were. Dale showed him the entrances to the mine haul roads and the places on blind curves where the width of the road between the bluff of the mesa edge and an acequia on the other side makes two passenger cars passing each other a hairy experience, let alone a car and an eighteen-wheeler or two eighteen-wheelers.

Mary and her husband had both been forced off the road by trucks bearing down on them. A truck nearly killed Mary's eighty-one-year-old mother. She had to drive off the road however she could. Dale told Pete Rahn these stories and others as they drove through our communities. He thought Rahn was receptive to our point of view and took to heart the hazards we faced from Baker's trucks. We hoped to work with him regarding safety issues on the road. Dale felt optimistic.

Dale moderated the meeting. Out of courtesy we allowed Rahn to speak first. As soon as he took the microphone we knew we had been sandbagged. His manner was arrogant, his words inflammatory. He said he didn't believe in weight limits on roads; he thought they ought to be open to anyone to use. He implied that if we insisted on maintaining the weight limit we might be sorry. Propane trucks, concrete trucks, and others that might exceed the load limit could be cited or denied access. My take was that he would see to it that the limit was enforced rigorously. He made no distinction between the occasional propane truck and mining trucks that ran all day, every day. Rahn told us that the decision about the road was his alone to make. He would let us know in thirty days. The truckers cheered.

Mary spoke next. Loud catcalls echoed from the truckers' area of the gym. Clearly, many of them had been drinking. I wondered if Baker had supplied the booze.

Wilbur Atencio, former governor of San Juan Pueblo, followed Mary. The truckers upped the level of their derision a notch. Wilbur stopped after saying a few words and stood with silent dignity. The room quieted a little. Wilbur said he had not come to be disrespected. He gave an impassioned plea for preservation of the petroglyphs. All of the Vecinos supporters applauded loudly when Wilbur finished. Wilbur was our hero of the moment.

Then Rose took the podium, her red hair flashing in the spotlight. The truckers increased their harassing behavior. My friend Elena Pérez who sat near Baker and his crowd said that Baker egged them on. When Rose began speaking one of Baker's guys yelled, "My dad used to see you swimming in the river naked as a jaybird." The truckers whistled and cheered. Isaac Martinez, the provocateur, was drunk. He was not a trucker but the unruly younger son of the man Baker had bought the mining land from. He worked for Baker occasionally. Rose continued with a strong voice in spite of the slur. She reinforced the theme that Vecinos did not want to deprive anyone of a job but that there were places to mine the materials that Baker needed—that we all needed—that were not in the midst of traditional farming communities.

Rose's neighbor Anita Ortega spoke next. She began to tell the story of trucks trying to pass each other in front of her house. The road is extremely narrow there. Across from Anita's house is a small historic capilla Rose had worked to put on the State Register of Cultural Properties. The side mirrors of the two trucks locked and the proximity of Anita's house made it almost impossible for the trucks to back up and disentangle.

The truckers in the audience launched into a new round of insults and hooting. No one could hear Anita. Tears rolled down her face. She couldn't finish her comments and sat down. Even though Anita was Hispana, I began to wonder if Baker was deliberately trying to insert racism into the agenda, as though Hispanos who sided with Anglos were traitors; as though Anglos protesting the trucks were just meddlesome outsiders; as though Baker the patrón was not an Anglo himself.

Vecinos members were pleased that two county officials as well as a representative from the Bureau of Land Management spoke in our favor. We had had a couple of meetings with people from the BLM about areas where Baker could mine on BLM land away from any community. We hoped that they might engineer a land swap with Baker. They would trade him a space to mine in exchange for some of the petroglyph sites he owned on the mesa. We thought the idea was the perfect solution. Getting Baker to agree was another matter.

At one point some of the truckers started yelling about why they were not allowed to speak. Dale Gardner decided it would be politic to let a few of them talk. Isaac Martinez took the microphone and informed us that Baker didn't pay minimum wage, he paid a dollar above minimum wage. As though that made George Baker eligible for sainthood. I thought that was a good example of Baker's miserliness, given the fact that the truckers got no benefits and minimum wage was execrably low. I was embarrassed for Isaac.

At our postmortem Vecinos agreed that the turnout for the meeting reflected huge support for our position. None of us were very optimistic about Rahn's decision. We could only hope that the safety issues would haunt him.

Lloyd had come to the meeting separately and left before me. I felt a bit fearful walking to my car. Some of the other women from Vecinos felt the same way. A few of the truckers lingered outside laughing in small groups. Rose had been harassed and others threatened by truckers in the past.

Three days later we had another meeting with the Bureau of Reclamation at my house. Harry had developed a list of nineteen questions that he wanted to maneuver Garry Rowe into answering in this face-to-face setting. He had spent many hours preparing for the meeting.

The first hour of the meeting went well, though Garry Rowe gave grudging answers. He was the best I had ever seen at saying nothing and taking all day to say it. People began to get antsy as he blathered on and on. I thought he was irritatingly arrogant, but not as bad as he had been at the first meeting.

After the first hour the meeting deteriorated. Three or four people made it impossible for Harry to keep moving down his list. They had lost patience with BOR and were unaware of Harry's finely tuned plan. A couple of people from the neighborhood began shouting questions and opinions, even one of our members who should have known better. I didn't realize he was having a meltdown. His face was red but he said nothing. About twenty minutes after losing control of the meeting Harry got up and left. I was surprised and a little alarmed. The meeting continued another hour without much focus.

Three days later Dale Gardener got a letter from Harry saying he no longer wanted to be a member of Vecinos. He mentioned that he had written 140 letters for us, devoted endless hours to our cause, and had been waiting ten months to get answers to some of the questions he had posed to Garry Rowe. Harry said he left the meeting out of frustration, embarrassment, and disappointment. Given the way the meeting got off track he felt he had nothing more to offer us.

Harry had quit once before a few months earlier over another issue. That time I cried and went into a deep funk. I felt I could not continue the struggle without Harry's help. I wrote him a long, heart-wrenching letter praising him and emphasizing how irreplaceable he was and pleaded with him to reconsider. From the beginning I understood Harry wanted to be in control of all our actions regarding BOR. Harry was irreplaceable because of his knowledge of the Bureau of Reclamation. I willingly played the game his way.

This time his departure made me sad, but I didn't feel like it was the end of the world. I wrote him a letter thanking him for everything he had done and encouraging him to reconsider even though I sensed he would not. He had developed a health problem that was worrying him.

By then I had been waging war against Baker full tilt for almost a year. I was so tired I didn't have much fight left in me. And we had won some battles. At the meeting one of Rowe's staffers assured me that they would avoid doing business with Baker in the future if possible. He was too much of a headache.

Lloyd sailed his boat to Hawaii that spring with the help of the boat's builder and a couple of other guys. The voyage was the culmination of a long-standing dream. The trip turned out to be a slog most of the way. Leaden clouds, choppy seas, and frequent squalls. Not the kind of passage Lloyd had envisioned. Still, he reveled in the experience and enjoyed every minute. The boat had landed on the island of Hawaii. Lloyd spent some time getting to know the Big Island before he returned home. He planned to go back in the fall and at some point sail the boat to other islands in the Hawaiian chain.

In May Lloyd and I had a housewarming party. The portal still had a dirt floor rather than the flagstone we planned and landscaping remained to be completed, but we wanted to celebrate the completion of the house and invite friends and neighbors to have a look. I bought some pansies and geraniums for spots of outside color.

The day was windless and sunny, the temperature perfect. We borrowed tables and chairs and set them up on the portal. I had a caterer come and deal with the food. I didn't want to be shuffling back and forth to the kitchen during the party. More than fifty people came. Neighbors, most of the guys who had been a part of the construction crew, including Ernie, and friends from Santa Fe. Several people brought kids, one who spent most of his time exercising the refrigerator's ice maker. Most people stayed a couple of hours or more. One of my petroglyph friends gave a tour for those who had not seen the glyphs. I gave endless tours of the house and explained the virtues of straw-bale building. The little bathroom with the corrugated metal shower proved to be one of the favorite features of the house. Many people were enamored of the mud-plastered walls and the kitchen cabinets Ernie had built. Everyone agreed that my kitchen view is world-class.

By then the pain and stress of construction had begun to fade and I too could finally enjoy the warmth and simple beauty of my home. Lloyd smiled humbly at the legions of compliments. I spent a lot of time talking to neighbors about the status of the fight with Baker and what came next.

Sometimes in the all-consuming battle with the Bureau of Reclamation and NMDOT I lost sight of my connection to the petroglyphs and the serenity of the place. I had come here for a simpler, more peaceful life. That goal had eluded me except for short periods in the first few years. But now and then I experienced a numinous moment—the full moon hanging like a communion host over the Sangres, a vast canvas of clouds against the piercing blue sky of a summer afternoon, revisiting a favorite petroglyph on smooth stone like the sun-headed image that spoke to me with all the force of words. Those moments kept me from going over the edge or back to California.

Such moments were a trade-off with the grinding fatigue, lost sleep, and frequent despair of the last year. The struggle aged me. I felt like a forty-year-old when we came here. Now, after a bad day, I felt eighty. Most days I was Lady Sisyphus rolling the boulder back up the damned hill with a bad back and aching shoulders. But every morning I took up the task again.

After Harry's departure in early 1998 Vecinos and I continued the row with Rowe and others from the Bureau of Reclamation, but the flow of letters slowed. Later in 1998 and early 1999 seeds we had planted began bearing fruit. In June we sent BOR a copy of an administrative order issued against Baker by the Environmental Protection Agency because he had not applied for a storm-water runoff permit.

We asked Charles Calhoun for information about BOR's long-range regional planning, knowing from Harry that they scheduled several years ahead. We wanted to know if any contracts were on the books for the mesa in the next five years. Calhoun said there were none.

Over the next year the Bureau of Reclamation made changes to its manual and procedures in compliance with the issues brought forward in Letty Belin's January 1998 letter and in another letter from her in November of that year. We received copies of the letters BOR wrote in March of 1999 to Belin and the State Historic Preservation Office outlining those changes. Those two documents reassured me that if Baker were ever to receive another contract from BOR the playing field would be different.

A letter Belin wrote to the Department of the Interior's solicitor Elaine England at the end of November 1998 was the most reassuring piece of paper to emerge from our whole ordeal. She enclosed a July 1998 decision in the case of *Hopi Tribe v. the Federal Highway Administration* in Phoenix. The case involved a similar situation to the one on our mesa, i.e., a federal agency's responsibility regarding historic properties. The judge ruled that federal agencies are responsible for "off-site historic properties for which an adverse effect is reasonably foreseeable." That decision was as close to having something set in concrete regarding protection of the petroglyphs and historic sites where federal contracts are involved as we could reasonably hope to achieve. Nobody buys riprap in quantity but the Bureau of Reclamation, the Corps of Engineers, and highway departments. If mining was ever going to be done on the mesa again, I knew there were laws to regulate the process. Perhaps Baker's aversion to compliance was my best protection.

After our meeting with Pete Rahn, Vecinos del Rio stepped up our letter-writing campaign regarding NMDOT, including letters to newspapers. We kept hitting Rahn with the words he used in the variance he had granted Baker, that his "first responsibility was safety to the public." Pete Rahn, after long delays in the decision-making process, decided not to scrap the load limit on SR 582—at least for the time being.

After almost a year of the assault of mining and the hazards of eighteen-wheelers on our road, and nearly two years of fighting these nightmares, the mesa and the small communities at its base settled back into the bucolic state from which they had been so rudely awakened.

Our peace was short lived. Baker rode over San Juan Pueblo's edict banning eighteen-wheel trucks from their land. He resumed mining gravel in Rose's neighborhood. Even she was unable to find out why the pueblo changed its policy. And Baker began a new mine in a village across the river, his second in that locale. Vecinos did its best to see that what law existed regarding gravel mining was enforced.

In 1998 Vecinos began working with Rio Arriba County, Baker, the BLM, and a representative from the governor's office to write sand, gravel, and riprap mining regulations for the county. Baker dragged his feet every step of the way, but in 1999, over his strenuous objections, our county commissioners courageously voted the regulations into law. The issue then became enforcement of those regulations. That is a story unto itself.

If it weren't for Baker I would have quietly enjoyed the land and the petroglyphs. I would not have become so involved in my community. I would have created more art. That was not to be. I like the Chinese proverb, "Be careful what you wish for." I wished to be the steward of this place. I got my intemperate wish, but the baggage that came with it has often been too heavy. I have had to drag the load much of the way.

Baker has robbed me of sleep, years of my life, and pieces of my sanity. In return I got a group of amazing people who care about protecting this special place. Without them I could not have achieved an iota of what we have accomplished together. Maybe it's a fair trade. Shall I say, "Thank you, George Baker"?

I hope Baker is the last of his kind, the last bearer of the Wild West mentality that says you can do whatever you want on your own property regardless of the effect on your neighbor and your community. He sees me as a troublesome "newcomer." In a sense I am. One's family has to live here two hundred years for one to qualify as a local. That's okay. I'll take the label. Most of my neighbors, Hispano, Indian, and Anglo, understand that Baker's way of doing things is a relic of another time.

I fantasize that Baker will have an epiphany. That he will wake up one day soon and realize that his only enduring legacy consists of large, ugly scars on the earth. I keep hoping that he will grow a little in his soul and do what's right: stop mining in villages and start protecting his petroglyphs and their context. He is said to value the big Awanyu and the magnificent upside-down figure. I hope that is true. I hope he will protect those glyphs and the thousands of others he owns by putting his land into a protective easement or donating the property to a conservation group.

Long after Baker's last truck went down the road, the last letter of protest was mailed, the final touches put on the dream house, I suffered paralyzing fatigue and something like PTSD. Even small things like a door slamming sometimes made me go to pieces. One day in Santa Fe the summer following the end of the mining but before the "paper war" had ended, Lloyd and I pulled into a parking spot. I was on the passenger side. For unknown reasons my side window suddenly made a loud cracking noise and shattered into a thousand pieces. Even though I was unhurt I became hysterical, which is not my style. A quarter of an hour passed before I was able to get hold of myself. Lloyd had never seen me in such a state—I had never been in such a state—and didn't know what to do. Long-term stress had clearly taken a toll. I had allowed myself to take on more than my system could physically and psychologically tolerate over a long period. Health issues in subsequent years are testament to that. I paid dearly for not knowing my limits.

Do I have regrets? Absolutely. There have been days when I wished I had never heard of New Mexico or wished that Lloyd and I had bought a house in a quiet Santa Fe neighborhood where my experience would have been a little less "rich" and a lot less costly in terms of my energy and my life-force with which I have "paid" for my peerless, priceless time on the mesa. I came, I saw, I overextended. Would I do it again if I had known in 1992 what I know now? I don't think so.

Still, the place possesses me. I can no longer race up the hill to the Key Rock as I could on that first day on the mesa. The cartilage in my knees is gone, but the magic of the petroglyphs remains. The landscape and skyscapes awe me no less now than that first summer. The view from my kitchen window each day, each season, is a pure blessing. The land is my hard-won refuge. Beloved, boulder-strewn home.

Katherine Wells

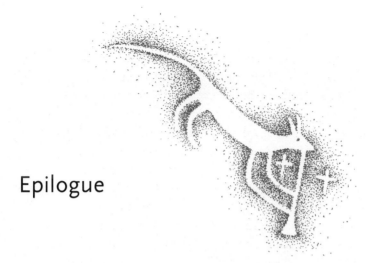

Epilogue

My partner, Lloyd Dennis, died on October 15, 2001. Because he knew death was coming, Lloyd had ample opportunity to put his affairs in order and he did so, except for the decision about his remains. Some days he talked of cremation. Other times he leaned toward burial on our land. Home burial is legal in New Mexico.

A month or so before Lloyd died he was leaning toward burial and thinking if he had the energy he would build himself a coffin. Something plain, probably pine. Then an idea he liked even better came to him. He would buy about ten yards of heavy canvas and, as he said, be "wrapped and tied like a tamale" and put into the ground. This was quintessential Lloyd.

Events overtook him and in the end his children decided the question of his remains. Because he loved both the high desert of New Mexico and the Pacific Ocean of his native California, they chose to have their father cremated and to spread half his ashes in each location.

The October day of Lloyd's outdoor memorial in New Mexico was beautiful beyond saying. The cottonwoods along the Rio Grande below our house were at the peak of golden perfection and blazed in the bright sun. The sky was piercingly blue with mounds of cumulus clouds. Lloyd's children built a small shrine near the house where we could gather with friends and neighbors overlooking the river.

The shrine consisted of a two-hundred-pound stone Lloyd had chosen for a project he wanted to do, a three-foot-high cross he made several years earlier from weathered lumber, an old serape from Mexico he had owned for decades, and many items that spoke of his passions and quirks: beloved fishing gear, favorite tools, a memento from his boat, some of the little clay blocks we used to build a model of our house, and an antique toy cement truck his daughter Michele had given him years earlier. On top of the shrine we mounted a silver fork because food was Lloyd's religion.

True to form the last act of Lloyd's life was food related. The end came suddenly after only a few days of intense pain. Friends came to help and five of his six children arrived before he died. Even with unlimited morphine it was hard to keep him comfortable that last day. He ate nothing but a couple of bites of oatmeal for breakfast. He was barely able to move. At dinnertime he refused food. I suggested he might want some ice cream later and mentioned that a friend had brought a freshly baked apple pie.

Around nine in the evening Lloyd's pain was under control and he seemed comfortable, though barely conscious. He was so close to death the aura of it hung in the air. I couldn't imagine where he was. I asked if he was ready for ice cream. Lloyd vaguely nodded and one of his daughters went into the kitchen to get some. Then I remembered the pie.

"Would you like some pie with the ice cream?" I asked. From somewhere deep inside Lloyd dredged up a last flash of his considerable personality, humor, and energy. In slurred speech he said, "I thought you'd never ask." Everyone in the room broke into laughter and tears at the same time. These were the last intelligible words Lloyd ever said.

The speed of Lloyd's ultimate decline was breathtaking. What truly amazed me though was that he seemed to hold himself together by grit alone until the very last grain was spent. Lloyd was a man who lived by his own lights and died by them, too.

The possibility of hospitalization was mentioned more than once his last couple of days. "What would I want to do that for?" he asked with contempt each time. I believe quite literally that Lloyd orchestrated his own exit. As his daughter Gwen said in her eulogy at the memorial service, "When it was time for living he lived to the hilt. When it was time to die, he lay down and did it with a minimum of fuss."

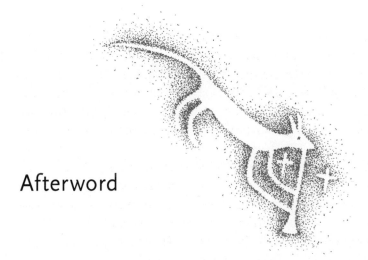

Afterword

Before the dust had settled from Baker's last truck I had become convinced that, ultimately, education is the only protection from him for the community and the petroglyphs. Local residents and others interested in petroglyphs would need opportunities to visit the site, learn about the glyphs, and participate in efforts to preserve this archaeological wonderland. I began to ponder what steps Vecinos del Rio and I could make in the direction of preservation. I talked with neighbors, friends, and petroglyph buffs.

Some measures were obvious. I thought perhaps the 188 acres Lloyd and I had bought would qualify for the National Register of Historic Places and the State Register of Cultural Properties. I obtained the application forms from SHPO. The National Register program offers no real protection for a site, but the designation has prestige and psychological value. I spent the next few months researching the information I needed and writing the lengthy text required. In July of 1999, SHPO approved the nomination for the National Register and conferred State Register status on the site. I received a letter of designation to the National Register from Washington, D.C., that September.

In the fall of 1999, I learned from Peggy Coyne, Vecinos del Rio's most active member, about a grant for $2,000 Vecinos del Rio could apply for from SHPO for a conservation project. What could we accomplish to help protect the petroglyphs with such a sum? I had long had the dream of recording all the petroglyphs on the mesa, but the job would be colossal. I suspected that $2,000 wouldn't even pay for the film and developing. We could, though, learn a bit about the magnitude of such a recording project and develop a better understanding of what we would be facing.

We submitted a proposal together with a support letter from San Juan Pueblo. I was happily surprised when the money was granted. We contracted with a local freelance archaeologist to help locate maps and determine where large concentrations of petroglyphs were, who owned them, how difficult the terrain was, and if gaining access would be a problem. At the end of the grant period we had a better sense of what an audacious project we were contemplating.

In the summer of 2001 I decided a logical first step toward beginning a program to protect and record the petroglyphs would be to organize a meeting and invite people interested in the glyphs to attend: locals, archaeologists, rock art buffs, and others from Santa Fe and Taos. We met in September under the sponsorship of Vecinos del Rio. About fifteen people attended the meeting. Among them was archaeologist and ethnobotanist Dr. Richard I. Ford of the University of Michigan, who has done most of his research in our area and would play a crucial role in the nascent project. The meeting convinced us that there was sufficient interest in the protection of the mesa to move ahead.

During the following winter I worked with Vecinos del Rio president Donna House to outline a plan. I obtained permission from a few landowners to record petroglyphs on their property and started investigating grant possibilities. We had already received several generous donations that enabled us to buy basic supplies and a couple of inexpensive pieces of equipment we would need.

The Vecinos del Rio members and I discussed ways to raise funds to support our proposed project. One idea was to create an "Adopt-a-Petroglyph" plan. I had "adopted" a whale for my son when he was a child and didn't see why the same idea couldn't transfer to petroglyphs. People who came on tours and cared about preserving rock art would, we hoped, adopt glyphs. We touted the idea as the perfect gift for the person who has everything.

We held a couple of group meetings at my house, which became the project's operations center. The first order of business was to write a mission/vision statement. By April we had a solid committee and decided to conduct a pilot recording program that summer, 2002. There was frequent discussion about the need for a part-time project coordinator. The job of orchestrating our activities and raising funds was growing by leaps and bounds. I was devoting most of my time to the endeavor, but felt I could not continue to do so indefinitely.

We decided to run the pilot program in July. Gearing up for the program was a mad scramble. We had to beg and borrow equipment. We also had to refine and produce recording forms, obtain Laboratory of Anthropology numbers, and resolve a host of other problems.

We had lengthy conversations concerning the enormous complexity and huge cost of developing a database we would build using GIS—Geographic Information System—to reference and map all the information collected while recording in the field. All petroglyph recording was now being done with GPS, and we would use GPS units borrowed from the Bureau of Land Management. Paul Williams, the BLM archaeologist in our area, became an important benefactor of the project.

There was endless discussion about the virtues of using traditional thirty-five-millimeter black-and-white photography versus joining the brave new world of digital cameras. Finally, digital won.

I suggested all the information be shared with San Juan Pueblo. Our program, which had become the Vecinos del Rio Mesa Prieta Petroglyph Project, would retain a copy. Each landowner would receive a copy of all the photos and information collected on his or her land as well as the associated database material.

For the pilot project we would record on BLM land on the north end of the mesa. I had envisioned youth from the local pueblos being a part of our project. The others on the committee embraced the idea and we decided to build a youth component into the pilot program. Our volunteers, including an elder from San Juan Pueblo who offered a blessing in Tewa every day, spent two weeks in July recording petroglyphs near the Rio Grande in the Embudo area. Youth from San Juan and other tribes worked alongside the adults. Paul Williams pronounced the program a success in terms of the number of glyphs recorded. We realized though, that we had a lot to learn.

In October 2002 we held a two-day training workshop for adult volunteers who wanted to learn how to be rock art recorders. About twenty bright, enthusiastic people crowded into my living room to learn the proper procedures. Each team would need an artist/recorder to sketch the petroglyphs and fill in the photo data sheets with information about them. The photographer had the job of taking a digital photo from the same angle as the artist's sketch and scouting for which petroglyphs should be recorded next. The team's mapper took GPS readings for each glyph and fed information to the recorder. Everyone helped with measurements and compass readings.

We had received permission to record a 250-acre parcel from a landowner who lived a few miles north of my property and planned to begin working there in the spring of 2003. The size of the parcel was daunting, as was the extreme ruggedness of the terrain. Candie and Lee Borduin, who had gone through recorder training, volunteered to tackle the first crucial and overwhelming job: to divide the land into reasonable-sized pieces for recording teams to work on. We assigned three or four teams to the parcel. Each team was free to work at times agreeable to its members.

In the fall of 2002, we received a request to have a group of Hopi-Tewa elders visit the petroglyphs on my site. They were from the village of Hano in Hopi, which is made up of descendents of people who fled the village of Pfioge on the other side of the Rio Grande when the Spanish arrived. Donna House, Tessie Naranjo from Santa Clara Pueblo, and I organized an afternoon tour. The group assembled at my house and we escorted them to petroglyph areas. We let them wander or be guided as they chose. It was great fun watching small groups of them gather around a petroglyph panel and discuss glyphs with animated gestures and emphatic voices in Tewa.

Around New Year's Day of 2003, I got an e-mail from James Chancellor, a friend who worked for the Eight Northern Indian Pueblos Council. He attached information about grants for projects involving youth available to Indian tribes from the National Park Service (NPS). James wondered if we might be interested in a joint project with the pueblo. I talked it over with Suzie Frazier, who had become my chief lieutenant in the project, and conferred with former San Juan Pueblo governor Herman Agoyo. Suzie and I thought a rock art recording program with pueblo youth working in conjunction with their elders to record petroglyphs would be an exciting project. Herman agreed. I wrote the text for the application while Suzie calculated the necessary budget numbers. Herman approved our work. The governor of San Juan Pueblo wrote the requisite support letter to accompany the weighty application.

By the spring of 2003 we had raised enough money through some small foundation grants and contributions to hire a part-time coordinator. We were fortunate to attract Beth Ann Sánchez, a young woman from my neighborhood who had just returned from the Peace Corps.

Shortly after Beth came to work for us we learned we had been awarded the grant and that San Juan Pueblo would receive $44,000 from the National Park Service. Tribal elders and young people would be paid to participate, as would a couple of support people from the pueblo. Beth would be paid from the grant for the time she spent coordinating the program and working with the youth and elders in the field. They would work on parcels of land a few miles north of the pueblo. We planned to begin the program in fall of 2003.

Before that project, Beth began her work with the Mesa Prieta Petroglyph Project by organizing our second annual Summer Youth Intern Program, scheduled for June of 2003. That second summer we were much better organized and equipped than we had been the first year. We recruited a dozen teenagers from area pueblos and Hispano communities. Several adult volunteers signed up to help as well.

The program began with a day of instruction under my carport, which offered some relief from the June sun. We started with a prayer offered in Tewa by Herman Agoyo. He then took the pueblo youth aside to an area with petroglyphs nearby for a few minutes. We assumed that he spoke to them about the glyphs from the pueblo point of view.

Early the following morning we ferried the troops to the recording site. The day was hot and cloudless. By 10:00 a.m. everyone was beginning to wilt as the temperature climbed toward one hundred degrees, but we kept working. We finished up in the field around noon every day and went to a picnic shelter by the river to eat lunch and talk about the day's work. A big topic of conversation that first day was the rattlesnake that Suzie had nearly stepped on.

On the last day of the program we took the group to the computer lab at Northern New Mexico Community College in Española. Under the guidance of department head Jeff Toomey each student got to enter the information and GPS locations of glyphs they had recorded into a mapping program called ArcView. The glyphs showed up as bright green dots on a three-dimensional map of the mesa. Then we had a little ceremony where we presented all of the students and adult volunteers certificates of participation and a hat embroidered with our project logo. Each student got a stipend check from the BLM.

In the fall of 2003, the Mesa Prieta Petroglyph Project was given the Youth Environmental Hope Award by the New Mexico Environmental Law Center honoring our Summer Youth Intern Program. At the awards ceremony the youngsters who went radiated pride when they spoke briefly of what they had learned in our program and why it was important. We have continued the Summer Youth Intern Program each successive year and have received widespread recognition for it. At the end of each two-week project we ask the students to evaluate the program. Their statements are always gratifying.

Under the terms of the NPS grant we garnered, Beth Ann Sánchez and a couple of volunteers began working with elders and youth from San Juan Pueblo to record petroglyphs on private land a few miles north of the pueblo in the fall of 2003. The young participants turned out to be talented recorders. A few had great drawing skills. They were sweet, resourceful, intelligent kids who were fun to be with. In the end a video was made about the project.

In early 2005, the idea of creating a curriculum about rock art for the area's public and pueblo schools began rolling around in my head. I presented the idea to our committee. Everyone liked the concept. We decided to approach Judy Chaddick, a local award-winning retired teacher who has a passion for petroglyphs, to work with us as a consultant. We had received our first significant grant from a local family foundation in the fall of 2004, which would provide us a modest amount of funds to develop such a project.

We began the long process of developing a curriculum for fourth- and seventh-grade students to complement their study of New Mexico history. Judy named the curriculum Discovering the Story of Mesa Prieta. With

Katherine Wells

the committee's input she developed classroom activities relating to petroglyphs that dovetailed with the State's required subject matter.

After a class completed the classroom activities it would have an opportunity to visit my site on the mesa for a field study day. The students would see petroglyphs, draw images of them, and observe things like relative patination, various image motifs, and glyphs from different time periods. They would hike the rugged terrain of the mesa and learn how to be safe in a new environment.

On a snowy day in January of 2007, we held a workshop to train our first teachers from public and pueblo schools to use the curriculum. They were very enthusiastic and made good suggestions.

That spring students from classes that had been exposed to the program came for field study days on the mesa. Their excitement was palpable. We discovered that many of the children had never been on a hike or had any significant outdoor experience. One girl got off the bus and looked at the first hill of the mesa as though viewing Mt. Everest. "Are we going up there?" she asked in a fearful voice. An hour later she was scampering up and down trails with complete confidence. The program continues to grow and we hope about three hundred youngsters will participate each year.

We have trained more volunteer recorders for our teams as needed. Since the digital photography and GPS units that we now use were not available when my site was recorded in 1993–1994, we had to rerecord my 188 acres. To leave that information out of our database would be like leaving all of the information about New England out of a database describing the United States. In 2005, the first teams were assigned to start rerecording my site. The project was completed in the summer of 2008.

In 2005 we also received permission to record a three-thousand-acre property that covers vast areas high on the mesa to the south of my property. We knew that the terrain would be very challenging and that teams would often have to hike an hour or more to areas where there are images to record. Out teams began work there in 2007. It may take decades to finish the job, but the tract represents an important part of the entire project.

There are many parcels of private land of various sizes with petroglyphs on the mesa that have not been recorded. The biggest is the seven thousand acres of land belonging to Baker. Because Vecinos del Rio has fought four of Baker's mines in our immediate area, he is unwilling to allow us to record his huge inventory of petroglyphs. A Vecinos del Rio member who has known him for many years and has a cordial relationship with him volunteered to talk to Baker. He responded that he would let us record if Vecinos del Rio promised to stop contesting his mining activities. The organization only protests Baker's activities that are illegal and will continue to do so. I continue to hope that Baker change his mind.

In January of 2006 we held a celebration of the work we had completed up to that time. We presented a copy of all the information we had collected to the landowners whose property we had recorded and to Herman Agoyo for the pueblo's archives.

Suzie Frazier and I presented Beth Ann, who directed much of the recording, with a gift certificate for books. She had done an outstanding job, but left us in the summer of 2006 to pursue a teaching career.

I talked Suzie into taking over the coordinator's job. She had been slowly phasing out of her previous occupation and devoting more and more hours to the project. Her organizational skills, energy, and passion for the program have added immeasurably to what we have achieved.

In 1996, I had bought Lloyd out of his share of our jointly owned property. Because of his prostate cancer prognosis we both assumed that I would outlive him. Since our early years in New Mexico I had been thinking about how I could legally protect the petroglyphs on my site. I felt it was important to do what I could. I entertained various schemes and weighed the possibilities financially. I researched ways that land can be protected.

In 2000 I met with Jim Walker from The Archaeological Conservancy and decided that I would give that organization an easement on all of my land except a three-acre parcel around my house, a one-and-a-half acre parcel around the rental house, and another small lot. The Conservancy will protect the petroglyphs in perpetuity from mining, grazing, and development. In 2007, I gave the Conservancy the land outright. They now own 156.01 acres.

The Mesa Prieta Petroglyph Project has partnered with The Archaeological Conservancy and the Petroglyph Project now manages the site. In 2007 Candie Borduin organized a Site Steward program for what has come to be known as the Wells Petroglyph Preserve. We trained a dozen volunteer Stewards who make monthly visits to areas of the property assigned to them and report any vandalism or intrusions they discover.

My original impulse was to keep a low profile for the site, thinking that was the best way to protect it. When Baker began mining on my boundary I changed my mind. The local community and the "petroglyph world" needed to know about its importance. Thus began my long odyssey to involve others in its protection. I began to get requests from pueblo tribal members, archaeological groups, teachers, hiking clubs, and others for tours. There has always been a steady stream of archaeologists, photographers, and dedicated petroglyph buffs wanting to visit. In 2005 the Petroglyph Project began offering four tours a year that are open to the public—two in the fall and two in the spring. In 2007 we trained a cadre of volunteer docents, mostly local people, to assist with and conduct tours. We encourage visitors to make donations to the Mesa Prieta Petroglyph Project or to "adopt" petroglyphs to help us cover our costs. Many have been very generous.

Though the project has been a colossal amount of work, it has been a labor of love. One of the biggest benefits has been that the endeavor has allowed me to get to know and work with my neighbors, who have supported the project in countless ways. It has given me an opportunity to meet and work with world-class archaeologists, countless petroglyph aficionados, and scores of other wonderful people who share my interest.

I am constantly astonished at the dedication, intelligence, wisdom, generosity, kindness, enthusiasm, and toughness of the dozens of volunteers who have worked with the project over the years. Many who have been involved since the beginning will continue to work with us until the last bit of information has been entered into the database. We have a ninety-one-year-old still working on a recording team who doesn't care if he keels over on the job. He'll die doing what he loves. Many of our volunteers are just that devoted. I wish there were some way I could convey to them all how deeply I appreciate them. They are the heart and soul of the project, the ones to whom we should all be grateful for their devotion and perseverance in protecting the little slice of history represented by the marvelous and mysterious images left on the mesa's rocks.

Another of my rewards for working to protect the petroglyphs came in the form of recognition from ARARA, the American Rock Art Research Association, a national organization dedicated to the study and protection of rock art in all parts of our nation. In 2005 they named me their Conservation and Preservation Award winner. I went to their annual conference in Reno, Nevada, to accept the award. It felt wonderful to be honored by the world's largest organization of people who share my love of petroglyphs. In 2008 ARARA created a new Education Award. The Mesa Prieta Petroglyph Project was the first recipient of the honor.

Perhaps my most satisfying reward came in September 2006. The project was awarded a prestigious Piñon Award by the Santa Fe Community Foundation. The honor is a stamp of approval for the crème de la crème of Santa Fe-area nonprofit organizations. To receive the award I stood on the stage at the Lensic Theater beside several of the project's most devoted volunteers and benefactors and half a dozen smiling but nervous Native American and Hispano youngsters who have participated in our Summer Youth Internship Program. We all felt enormously proud.

Our effort has succeeded, not only because of the dedication of our volunteers, but also because of the amazing generosity of several private and public foundations and many individual "angel" donors. My hope is that all those who have helped financially feel their gifts are a good investment in the future.

The petroglyph committee's plan is to continue recording petroglyphs until the last one is recorded. Entering all the information we have collected thus far, and all that we will collect in the future into our database, will take a concerted effort on an ongoing basis. It will be a great day when we deliver the "whole enchilada" to ARMS. If there is a heaven with bells, they will ring out on that day.

I hope that the youth education elements of our program will continue and expand to include more and more children. All of the youngsters who live in view of the mesa deserve to have an opportunity to learn about its history and their connection to it. They should have an opportunity to visit and develop a sense of their ancestral relationship with the massive landform and its cultural treasures in their midst.

Postscript: In December of 2008, a serendipitous event occurred. A supporter of the Petroglyph Project persuaded George Baker to give us permission to record the petroglyphs on his land without preconditions. The gesture will benefit the local community and the world of archaeology. I am grateful to Baker for his change of heart.

For more information about the

Mesa Prieta Petroglyph Project

email mesaprieta@cybermesa.com.